'Whaddaya Know?'

AF583908

‘Whaddaya Know?’

Writings for Syd Harrex

edited by

RON BLABER

Wakefield
Press

Wakefield Press
16 Rose Street
Mile End
South Australia 5031
www.wakefieldpress.com.au

First published 2015

Copyright © in this compilation Ron Blaber 2015;
copyright in individual contributions remains
with the respective authors

All rights reserved. This book is copyright. Apart from any fair dealing for the purposes of private study, research, criticism or review, as permitted under the Copyright Act, no part may be reproduced without written permission. Enquiries should be addressed to the publisher.

Cover designed by Michael Deves, Wakefield Press
Typeset by Wakefield Press
Printed in Australia by Griffin Digital, Adelaide

National Library of Australia Cataloguing-in-Publication entry

Title:	'Whaddaya know?': writings for Syd Harrex / edited by Ron Blaber.
ISBN:	978 1 74305 340 9 (paperback).
Subjects:	Harrex, S.C. Festschriften – Australia. College teachers – South Australia – Adelaide. Commonwealth literature (English) – Study and teaching – South Australia – Adelaide. English literature – Study and teaching – South Australia – Adelaide.
Other Creators/ Contributors:	Blaber, Ronald Leslie, editor.
Dewey Number:	828.4

Contents

PAST WRITINGS

IN MEMORIAM

SYD HARREX
1935 – 2015

Our good friend, colleague and mentor, Syd Harrex, died in the middle of 2015, just short of the fifty-year anniversary of his starting work at a new university in South Australia, soon to be known as Flinders University. Syd was not just a founding member of staff at Flinders, he created a vital and far-reaching research centre and network of teachers and scholars, some of whose words appear in this volume. He connected many of us to a wider world.

Vale, Sydji.

Rick Hosking

Acknowledgements

The contributions of Satendra Nandan, Vincent O'Sullivan, Murray Bramwell and Brian Matthews were previously published and are reprinted here with permission of the authors.

Ron Shapiro's 'The Darville/Demidenko Affair: Jew and Anti-Jew in Australian Fiction' first appeared in *Westerly* and is reprinted here with permission of the journal.

I would like to thank all the contributors and those who were approached but were unable to make a contribution at this time, much to their own disappointment. All acknowledged the appropriateness of honouring Syd Harrex, his contribution to, and standing in, the field of New Literatures in English.

I would like to thank the Faculty of Humanities and the School of Media Culture and Creative Arts at Curtin University for the financial assistance in enabling this collection to come to fruition.

Ron Blaber

Whaddaya Know

RON BLABER
CURTIN UNIVERSITY

One should not really explain humour or jokes but the title of this collection does require some comment. The question 'Whaddaya know?' was a common utterance in the corridors and staff room of the Humanities building when I was a doctoral student in the English Department at Flinders University in South Australia. The question functioned phatically in much the same way as 'How'r' ya goin?' or 'G'day': it was part of everyone's every day. The response was more telling, more important. The response to the question was invariably 'Fuck all' or perhaps 'Bugger all' followed by a smile or a laugh. The ritual exchange was repeated countless times and perhaps seems trivial but it signified a collegiality and, paradoxically, an understanding that we really didn't know anything much – at least at one level. That was why we there: pursuing research in what were then regarded as marginal or peripheral fields of investigation – peripheral because they were relatively new or because they had fallen out of fashion and had become residual to the dominant fields of literary study. Above all it was a different and exciting time.

The 1960s was marked by a significant expansion of the tertiary education sector. Flinders University was created in 1966. Its foundation represented a number of opportunities. Importantly, Flinders, along with other new universities, was part of a push to provide greater access to people who might not otherwise have considered going to university. Further, such developments also represented an opportunity to open up syllabi and curricula. In other words Flinders did not merely replicate the University of Adelaide in Adelaide's southern suburbs. Now nearly 50 years after its establishment, it would be a hard to dispute Flinders' success and the fact it has developed an enviable reputation in terms of the innovation and quality of its research and teaching.

For the fledgling School of Literature and Language, Flinders offered the opportunity not only to provide courses in traditional literary studies but also to explore some of the newer fields of study. In a very short time the English Department had developed particular strengths in Australian literary studies and Commonwealth Literary Studies, or as Syd Harrex would have it, and as his students and colleagues embraced it, New Literatures in English.

Through the guidance and patience of Syd Harrex, some 11 years after the establishment of the university, the English Department established the Centre for Research in New Literatures in English. The Centre promoted research into the literatures of India, Africa, the Caribbean, Canada and Australia, and other literature written in English. The acronym, CRNLE, generates a number of homonymic associations. As 'kernel' it signifies something foundational, central, developmental and creative; as 'colonel', it plays out a joke in terms of a claim to authority against a problematic relationship to history of colonialism. And it is this playfulness that underscores the wit, seriousness and sophistication of the research that is the hallmark of the work carried out by CRNLE.

A key moment in the history of CRNLE occurs 2 years after its foundation: 1979 sees the appearance of the *CRNLE Reviews Journal*. The Journal is typical of the creativity and risk taking associated with the Centre. A reviews journal, dedicated to reviewing new writing, both creative and critical, is a risk because one can never be sure whether it will find a niche in a saturated academic-journal market, or, for that matter, find contributors willing to give up time to review material. The reviews journal met with remarkable success, running from 1979 through to 1995. The number of contributors runs into the hundreds, if not thousand. As most will know, the review is undervalued but complex genre. The review is a highly disciplined form and an important vehicle to hone writing and critical thinking skills, especially for early career academics The relationship between the journal and contributors was of mutual benefit. On the one hand the journal gained from the calibre and reputations of its contributors; and on the other hand, I believe contributors benefitted from the discipline the form of the review offered. As part of this collection, I have included samples from the Journal. The success of the Journal afforded the Centre the opportunity to explore other types of publication, for example author and regional studies. This collection includes Dorothy Jones's fine essay on the work of Kamala Das.

But a question still remains: Why 'New Literatures in English'? In one sense the term New Literatures in English took into account that literatures written in English was much broader than literatures caught up in paradigm debates about the theoretical and political differences between the understandings of 'colonialism' and 'post(-)colonialism'. This is not to suggest that those working in the field were not aware of the political significance, importance of the literature with which they were engaged, rather the questions were of a slightly different nature but nevertheless informed by debates about the moment of 'colonialism'/'postcolonialism', particularly given the diversity of the 'colonial' experience both for the coloniser and the colonised.

Perhaps the term New Literatures in English operates within an older literary critical frame, one attentive to forms of representation and typicality wherein narrative informs the reader of specific instantiations not only of the experience and politics of difference, but also highly individualised narratives that appear only indirectly related to the politics of colonialism – on can consider here the work of R.K. Narayan and his superbly crafted world of Malgudi as compared to, say, the politically charged work of N'gugi wa Thiongo or perhaps to the postmodernist working of Salman Rushdie. The term 'New Literatures in English' endeavours to embrace and engage with the personal, the political and aesthetic dimensions of cross-cultural encounter. It was the complexity of this engagement that was absolutely crucial to Syd Harrex's own work and to others' work he helped mentor.

When one reads Syd's work, be it his criticism or poetry, or when one encounters his conference presentations and discussions, it is clear that the reader or audience is in the presence of a fine sensibility. Syd has a marvellous capacity to address a 'question', a 'problem', dare I say a 'problematic'. For example in the introduction to his collection *The Fire and the Offering*, Syd addresses the question of Indian Writing in English:

> ... the present book has been written in the awareness that Indian writing in English has emerged out of a confusion of cultural con-texts: the English, French and American Literary traditions, the Russian novel, literary modernism, Commonwealth writing, the Indian classical tradition, the Indian vernacular literatures, and the modern concept of 'Indian Literature'. But, in view of the impossible difficulties involved in examining the Indian novel in English in terms of all there complex backgrounds, especially at a time when the development and assessment of the novel are still relatively provisional, the ensuing discussion is conceived within a modest but hopefully useful framework. This framework, however, contains enough interesting problems and novels to engage the serious attention both of the authors and the readers of Indian fiction in English. (3)

Modest. Confident. Aware. The two volume collection provides astute readings of, among others, Mulk Raj Anand, Khushwant Singh, Kamala Markandaya, R.K. Narayan and G.V. Desani. While the above quotation points to a general understanding of 'interesting problems', Syd provides great insight into the specific. Writing of Kamala Das's use of English, he asserts.

> ... because she uses English, she sees herself addressing a diverse audience ranging from foreigners and Indians who do not know her to those who that know her well. She defines her speech in Indian-English in defence of a natural poetic; and it is a natural poetic, in the sense that her language is what has simply evolved along with her personality, and in the sense that she has Indianised the obvious borrowings of 'influence' out of existence. (*The Writer's Sense of the Past*, 63).

While these are indicative of Syd's critical work and insight to issues associate with New Literatures in English, there is an important essay, perhaps one that might be regarded as minor within Syd's work but one that points to his role as mentor. In his essay 'The Fascination of What's Difficult', Syd pays tribute and makes use of students' responses to Raja Rao. The essay is at once an investigation into the interpretation of a particular author, but also an interpretation of what it means to read and teach New Literatures in English:

> Teachers and students of literature have much to learn from each other, and many an article has been born out of tuto-rial discussion. The present essay is a personal record of such processes, and at-tempts to collate some unpublished inter-pretations of The Serpent and the Rope. Share with the student authors of these 'interpretations' the view that Raja Rao's novel belongs in that class of imaginative work which stimulates a variety (conflicting as well as complementary) of critical response. This conviction informs my commentary from the outset and is itself a critical judgement, for works of literature devoid of artistic merit cannot produce the kind of diverse depth of group discussion on which I will be focusing my attention. (178)

As a scholar and mentor, Syd was generous and supportive, ensuring that his colleagues and students achieved their very best. But Syd is more than that, as the contributions from Rick Hosking and Brian Matthews attest. However, the question remains: What do we know about Syd?

Texts cited

Syd Harrex, *The Fire and the Offering: The English-Language Novel of India 1935-1970*, 2 Volumes. (Calcutta, India: Writers Workshop, 1977).

Syd Harrex, 'The Strange Case of Matthew Arnold in a Sari or the Past as Prelude to Kamal Das', in *The Writer's Sense of the Past*, ed. Kirpal Singh, (Singapore: Singapore National Press,1987).

Syd Harrex, 'The Fascination of What's Difficult: Some Student Responses to Raja Rao', in *Indo-English Literature* ed. K.K. Sharma, (Ghaziabad, India: Vimal Prakashan, 1977)

Syd Harrex

RICK HOSKING
FLINDERS UNIVERSITY

Teacher, colleague, mate: Sydji, the honorific goes way back, intended and heartfelt.

I was in Syd's first class in the School of Language and Literature at Flinders; I met my wife Sue in one of his tutorials. In the mid-1960s we knew Syd as a teacher of poetry and of American Literature; his MA had been awarded for a study of the Californian poet Robinson Jeffers. One of our first dinner parties was marked by debate about *Huckleberry Finn* that lasted for days and was still raging at the pub a week later.

It was the first time we had seen Syd's hairstyle that gave him the suggestion of the bodgie, the two-bob lair. A little later on he returned from an early study leave in a safari suit; for years after he always seemed a little taken aback when someone insisted that he should turn up for a book launch or other CRNLE event in *that* safari suit.

Syd was finishing his PhD in those early years at Flinders: even as we were reading and arguing about Jeffers, Hart Crane, Henry James and Mark Twain, he was beginning to turn his attention to Indian writing in English, beginning to define what he would go on to call the 'New Literatures in English'. A decade or so later he would establish the Centre for the Study of the New Literatures in English in what had become by then the School of Humanities at Flinders, CRNLE for short, the first postcolonial research centre in the world. Some people called it 'CR'NLEE', the stress on the first syllable. Syd worked harder than anyone I have worked with to 'network', as they call it these days, building relationships between institutions, educational systems, colleagues and nations. A colleague, a Head of Faculty no less, had her bag stolen in Changi Airport in Singapore, her passport and money gone, no way of identifying herself. She rang the Australian High Commission and spoke to the officer on duty. When he heard she was from Flinders, he asked her if she knew Syd Harrex (and Rick Hosking, the author adds modestly). Syd had worked on developing long-term relationships and cultural exchanges between Indian and Australian universities; the officer on duty's previous posting had been Cultural Attaché in New Delhi.

Travelling companion. In 1983 I went to South East Asia and India for the first time with Syd and his wife Jane. Syd delivered a public lecture in a very flash hotel in Kuala Lumpur, with the ebullient Salleh Ben Joned snoring noisily in the front row but then awakening to engage with Syd and other members of the audience in animated discussion. They had first met at the University of Tasmania; perhaps Salleh picked up a little of the lair from Syd.

We visited Calcutta to meet the publisher, poet and professor Purushottama (P.) Lal, who had published Syd's PhD thesis and, in the years that followed, several volumes of Syd's poetry. We were invited to attend an evening of *Gaudiya Nritya*, the Bengali school of Indian classical dance, but many of the audience – both men and women – were restless and preoccupied, with several holding transistor radios to the ears or fiddling with earphones. With the fall of each West Indian wicket a wonderful wave washed around the audience, with some occasional elbowing from sari-clad wives. It was the night India won the 1983 World Cup: Calcutta later that night was extraordinary. We heard later that what we took for firecrackers was in fact gunfire.

I learned during that trip that Syd (and Jane) were not ones for early rising. In Calcutta I had discovered an alley at the back of the hotel where the local boys played cricket, so to pass the time I would umpire the scratch matches and advise on bowling in-swingers. I count the morning after the 1983 world cup win as one of the great moments in my life; Sydji might have been there if he had the habit of early rising. One of the young men asked me if I was Dennis Lillee.

After Calcutta, I travelled with Syd and Jane to Mysore; it was my first visit to Dhvanyaloka, the research centre established by Prof C.D. Narasimhaiah (CDN) in what were in those days the rural outskirts of Mysore. Like Syd, CDN enjoyed legendary status as a pioneer of what CDN called 'Commonwealth Literature'. There were many conversations on CDN's verandah about what the young folk were already calling 'postcolonial literature', CDN handing out Trichy cigars and splashing whisky in glasses. CDN told us that night that during the war when Winston Churchill could not get a steady supply of Cuban cigars he turned to the cigar rollers of Trichinapoly (now Tiruchirapalli) near Madras: these cigars, he insisted, are from the same factory. Syd used to enjoy a good cigar back then.

Conferenceville. How can I forget travelling with Syd, Brian Matthews and Adrian Caesar to an early Association for the Study of Australian Literature (ASAL) conference in Newcastle, New South Wales. Syd had been asked to chair a keynote address by Brian, but Sydji had a long memory, a recollection of Brian taking most of the allocated time at an EACLALS conference six months before in Malta. Syd began the introduction, Brian sitting modestly behind the podium, staring off into middle distance, no doubt rehearsing his first joke. Syd then explored in great and often minute detail every nuance of Brian's reputation, publications, research profile, joke-telling ability and inexplicable football team support (St Kilda). After fifteen minutes or so Brian picked up his chair and left the lecture theatre, only returning to present his paper when the laughter had subsided.

Syd at a reading in 1995, organised as part of another ASAL conference at a winery in South Australia's Southern Vales. The headline guest was Helen Demidenko, as she was known then; the previous day she had won the Australian Literature

Society's Gold Medal for *The Hand that Signed the Paper.* She was accompanied by a very blonde and taciturn young man who, she briskly informed us, was her minder, darkly suggesting she needed a bodyguard in case the Zionists attempted to take her out in the badlands of McLaren Flat. After the reading, the lunch and a brief attempt to teach the stayers some Ukrainian folk dancing from the star turn, a group of organisers gathered to sample a few bullsblood reds from the winery. Syd was rather quieter than usual, and out of the blue he called our soon-to-be-infamous guest 'a carnal fraud', to revive old Joe Furphy's turn of phrase. We decided to call an end to the lunch; while I took Syd home, Helen Demidenko and the taciturn blonde set off back to the city into a national and international furore.

Another vivid memory of Syd on yet another trip to India. We were standing in front of a Mysore shop that cheerfully announced that a pilewallah inside would have a crack at curing any case of hemorrhoids. Syd's hand fluttered over his backside, as he waited for me to take the photo.

Another trip to one of CDN's conferences, involving an afternoon drive from Chennai to Mysore. The vehicle, an Ambassador, had seen better days, and beyond Bangalore it was clear we would battle to reach Mysore. We limped along, the driverwallah jumping out every now and again to lift and bonnet and jiggle a few high-tension leads. Just before midnight and just a few miles out of Bangalore, the car gave up the ghost. All we could do was abandon the car and driver, shoulder our luggage and hitch through the dark. We did not have long to wait; a bus stopped, and we drove in style down to Mysore sitting in the back of the bus fending off questions about various members of the Australian cricket team and finding sensible answers to determined questioning about why Bollywood actors seemed not to be household names in Australia.

I taught with Syd in the Department of English at Flinders for over a decade, team-teaching both postcolonial literatures but more usually creative writing, the first undergraduate university creative writing course offered in South Australia. I got to work with Syd as a teacher at very close hand. While I would always insist that I do the jokes, it was very clear after just a few weeks of teaching that Syd brought an even temperament, unfailing good humour and a sprawling knowledge of the craft of literary studies to every class. At Syd's suggestion we called our course 'the craft and culture of creative writing', pioneering the teaching of literary technique and establishing a methodology that I still believe to be 'best practice', as it is now called. Our students produced half a dozen anthologies over the decade. We came to realise that while we could encourage the creativity of our students, we could also teach them how poetry and fiction work.

There are other sides to the man. Against a very strong field, Vince O'Sullivan awarded Syd the Bronze Turd Award for Syd's wide-mouthed frog joke. Many of us still vividly remember the actions that accompanied the telling.

While Syd is a loyal Crows supporter, he holds strong views about a Tasmanian team in the AFL, and about how the solitary win for St Kilda in 1966 was *entirely* due to the backbone of Tasmanian players in that team. Football is another side to Syd: all those afternoons and evenings spent at Football Park, with Rajah Huilgol on Syd's left barracking in any one of several languages and offering betel nut to all present, with me on the right offering all kinds of stentorian advice to players, coaches, opposition supporters and anyone else interested. Silent Syd would sit in the middle, seemingly unmoved, hunched forward, intently watching. Given the size of his feet, Syd must have been a classy centre-half-forward in the old days at Sandy Bay and at Hobart High.

A final Syd story. A colleague from Economics at Flinders University on his first conference trip to India presented his paper and waited for his first question. There were several young men lined up in the back row; there had been some animated discussion and argy-bargy in the group early in the presentation that the economist had observed, assuming that he had aroused the indignation of some members of the group. One of the young men raised his hand. With considerable solemnity, he framed his question. The question? Did the economist know Sydji Harrex.

Sydji Harrex: teacher, colleague, scholar, researcher, mate.

The Postcolonial Condition

REZA HAQUE
FLINDERS UNIVERSITY

Postcoloniality awaits consignment to oblivion.
Rukmini Bhaya Nair[1]

I posted a postcolonial poster
from the Postogola post office
in *puran* Dhaka, addressed to the right
reverend postmaster general in Portsmouth;
and eagerly waited for a kind reply.
To my absolute disappointment,
the (im)poster came back, a few weeks later,
with the stamps all missing; (old habit dies hard!)
At the upper right corner where the stamps
have been was written in a crooked hand –
not arrived yet – return it to sender.
The postcolonial poster now hangs
in my cool study, gathering grime,
the fringes yellowing with the passage of time.

Notes

This sonnet is dedicated to Syd Harrex who has done so much for the postcolonial cause. The poem has been accepted for publication in *Transnational Literature*, Vol. 5, No. 1.

1. *Rukmini Bhaya Nair, Lying on the Postcolonial Couch: The idea of Indifference* (Minneapolis: University of Minnesota Press, 2002) xi.

Walter Scott, the Bushranger, and the Bandit: Tales from Tasmania and Calabria

GRAHAM TULLOCH
FLINDERS UNIVERSITY

On 28 October 1820 Scott wrote to Lachlan Macquarie, then Governor of New South Wales, sending him a copy of his works and, it seems, asking in return for a copy of a book on Michael Howe, the Tasmanian bushranger. A year later, the letter and books having been delivered to him by Scott's protégé George Harper, Macquarie responded in a letter to Scott:

> I cannot express to you how much I feel pleased and flattered by your kind remembrance of me; and I feel particularly obliged and gratified by the honor you have done me in sending me a Present of your valuable and most interesting Works which I greatly prize, and hope one day ornament my Library with *in the Isle of Mull* where I should be most happy and proud to receive and welcome their Author. –
>
> I regret I have not now any thing to send you in return for this kindness that would be acceptable; but since you have asked for it, I now do myself the pleasure of sending you herewith the History of Michael Howe the Bush Ranger of Van Diemen's Land; but I hope soon to be able to collect for you a better History of him and the Bush-Ranging System in that Island. (ff. 165–66)

The book which Macquarie so apologetically provided was *Michael Howe, the last and worst of the Bush Rangers of Van Diemen's Land. Narrative of the Chief Atrocities committed by this Great Murderer and his Associates, during a Period of Six Years, in Van Diemen's Land. From authentic sources of information*, printed by Andrew Bent in Hobart in 1818. As I will show later, the language of the title ('last and worst ... atrocities') was fully justified: Howe was an extremely violent man, utterly ruthless in carrying out his crimes.

Some years later, in 1832, Scott was equally keen to locate a copy of an account of another violent criminal. On 15 April 1832, nearing the end of his sojourn in Naples, he recorded a story which he had been told by an apothecary, Roskilly (or, as he spelt it, Raxhealy), giving it the title 'Death of El Bizarro' (Scott, *Journal* 709–10). The story concerned the real-life bandit Francesco Moscato, known as Bizzarro because of his extraordinary and indeed truly bizarre cruelty. (Scott consistently uses a spelling with one *z* as in English, suggesting he strongly associated it with the meaning of the English word *bizarre* although, as it happens, Italian *bizzaro* has a wider range of meanings). As Scott records, he flourished in the Napoleonic era when the French under Joachim Murat ruled the kingdom of Naples and he collected a large 'gang of Banditti', to use Scott's term, with which he terrorised the country. It would appear that Scott sought to obtain a printed account of Moscato's life and he commissioned a young priest called Sticchini (we know only his surname) to find one, having earlier employed him in Naples to transcribe 'an old English manuscript of the Romance of Sir Bevis of Hampton, existing in the Royal library' (Lockhart 7: 351–52). However Sticchini reported that he had been unable to procure a copy even after applying to Roskilly and that all he could do was to send a collection of stories of brigandage in the kingdom of Naples (Sticchini f. 232). This collection is now, like the Howe booklet, in the Abbotsford library (*Catalogue* 340).

In Scott's brief account of the life and death of Moscato in his journal there are three particular incidents which I would like to highlight. Firstly there is the story of how il Bizzarro narrowly escaped capture:

> A French Colonel ... occupied the count[r]y of Bizarro with such success that he formd a cordon around him and his party

> and in[c]luded him between the folds of a military column. Well nigh driven to submit himself, the robber with his wife, a very handsome woman, and a child of a few months old, took a possession beneath the arch of an old bridge which crosst ther[e] and by an escape almost miraculous were not perceivd by a french strong party whom the french maintaind on the top of the arch. Night at length without a discovery which every moment might have made. When it became quite dark the Brigand, enjoining strictest silance on the female and child, resolve[d] to steal from his place of shelter and as the[y] issued forth kept his hand on the child's throat. But, as when they began to be moved the child naturally cried, its father in a rage stiffened his gripe so relentlessly that the poor infant never offended more in the same manner. (*Journal* 709)

Scott then goes on to explain how 'This horrid [s]in [du]ly led to the con[c]lusion of the Robber's life':

> after the death of the child the measure of his offence towards the unhappy mother was full to the brim and her thoughts became determined on revenge. One evening he took up his quarters for the night with the Precautions, but without the usual success. He had laid his carabine near him as usual and betaked himself to rest as usual when his partner arose from his side and ere he became sensible she had done so she seized [his weapon] and discharging [it] in his bosom ended at once his life and crimes. She finishd her work by cutting of[f] the Brigand's head and carrying it to the princ[i]pal town of the province where she deliverd it to the police and claimd and obtaind the reward attachd to his head which was paid accordingly. (710)

Finally he tells what he calls 'A story … nearly as horrible as the above respecting the cruelty of this Bandit which seems to enti[t]le him to the title of one of the most odious wretches of his name':

> A French officer who had been active in pursuit of him fell into his hands and was made to die [the death] of Marsyas

> or Saint Polycarp, that is, the period being the middle of summer, he was flayd alive and being smeard with honey was exposed to all the intolerable insects of a southern Sky. (710)

Moscato was indeed a ferociously violent and sadistic man. Contemporary accounts provide plenty of evidence of numerous barbaric acts such as tying a friend to a tree and having him eaten by his dogs; tying another man to a tree where he died of hunger, sunburn and insect bites (this is either same incident regarding a French officer as Scott recorded in his journal or a parallel case); cutting off the head of a man while still alive; eating the liver of two men he had captured; killing a priest by cutting off the ends of his limbs and throwing him over a cliff; sending the body of a supposed friend back to his family, chopped up in bits, after demanding a ransom, and so on and on (Prestera 173–81). Another account of his murder of his baby daughter, in an anonymous letter of 31 January 1811 in the Archivio di Stato di Napoli, claims that he killed her by battering her to pieces against a tree (quoted in Valente 182). We do not know whether Scott heard any of these other stories although the stories he does tell are barbaric enough for him to have understood that Moscato was an extremely violent man.

In fact Scott's interest in Moscato was more than passing. His final story, begun in Rome shortly after he left Naples, is a fictionalised account of Moscato's life in which the central figure is given the new name of Domenichino Castiliogne but retains the nickname of 'il Bizarro'. It includes what is for Scott an unusually violent scene. Domenichino and his associates murder the father and husband of a young woman and carry her off leaving behind a horrible token of their cruelty:

> though Antonio [the husband] had warning enough to start up and take to his defence, and either he or Monica appears to have wounded some one with his carabine, yet he, too, had fallen under the knives of numerous assailants, who seem to have meditated making a boast of their revenge. For they

> had cut the head of the unfortunate keeper's assistant from his body, and skewered fast to his forehead a placard to this purpose: 'Behold the head of Antonio Mutela, a teller of tales to His Majesty to the prejudice of his faithful subjects.'
>
> This head they doubtless intended to expose on some public part of the town. But time, or perhaps the cries of Monica, had interrupted them, though it had not prevented them from dragging with them one whom they had deprived of father and husband. (Scott, *Bizarro* 184)

I have not found anything resembling this particular story told regarding Moscato, although it may have been suggested to Scott's imagination by the story of his wife cutting off his head, but it certainly fits with Moscato's character.

What is particularly striking in this is Scott's manifest interest in an extremely violent person and his willingness to include an account of his violence in his story. In general Scott eschews violence in his fiction. There are, of course, notable exceptions such as the murder of Morris which filled the hero, Frank Osbaldistone, with 'sickening horror' in *Rob Roy* (267). There is also the killing of Oliver Proudfute in *The Fair Maid of Perth* and the particularly horrific and unprovoked murder of the Bishop of Liege in *Quentin Durward*. More typical perhaps of Scott is the threat of violence, of which *Ivanhoe* provides plenty of examples: leaving aside the implicit threat of rape which hangs over Rebecca and Rowena, there is Front-de-Boeuf's aborted attempt to roast Isaac and his threat to scalp Wamba. These two threats are in fact more horrifying than the actual murders in Scott's work and demonstrate the way in which extreme violence lurks beneath the surface of Scott's romance world but does not erupt into actuality. Nevertheless we are not accustomed to thinking of Scott as being interested in extreme violence – and yet extreme violence is exactly what Francesco Moscato practised, and Scott was clearly fascinated by this aspect of his character.

At this point it may be significant that Moscato was Scott's contemporary. The violence in *Rob Roy*, *Quentin Durward* and *The Fair Maid* is to some extent distanced by time, whereas the violent scene described in Scott's story *Bizarro* is said to have taken place 'in Calabria within these seven or eight years before the present date of 1832' (166). Indeed Scott in his fiction seems to have placed the events even closer to the present than he knew them as actual historical events to have taken place. Since Moscato's exploits were in the period of French rule, as Scott makes clear in the story, and French rule ended in 1815 they obviously occurred more than seven or eight years before 1832. Moscato actually died in 1810, twenty two years earlier. Scott seems, then, to have a particular interest in contemporary violence even to the extent of bringing it closer to the present than it actually was – which brings us back to the case of that other particularly violent contemporary outlaw, Michael Howe, who died only eight years after Moscato.

Whereas Scott first heard about Moscato in oral accounts, he would have first learnt about Howe from the May issue of the *Quarterly Review* where the booklet about his life was reviewed a few months before Scott wrote to Macquarie asking for a copy. The review was anonymous, as was the standard practice at the time, but it is attributed in the online *Quarterly Review Archive* to Barron Field who had spent ten years in Australia from 1814 to 1824 and was thus an appropriate choice as reviewer. There were several things that might have attracted Scott's attention in the review. The first does not relate to Scott's interest in violence, my subject here, but to his longstanding habit of book collecting. Field opens his review lightheartedly:

> This is the greatest literary curiosity that has yet come before us – the first child of the press of a state only fifteen years old. It will of course be reprinted here; – but our copy, the copy *penes nos*, is a genuine Caxton, *rarissimus* – nay more, it hath the title-page. Few impressions were thrown off at the Hobart Town Press, for the settlement does not greatly abound in readers; and we therefore recommend the Roxburghe Club to

> apply early for a copy, for this little book will assuredly be the 'Reynarde the Foxe' of Australian bibliomaniacs. (Field 73)

(The story of Michael Howe appears to have been the first non-government book published in Tasmania, then known, of course, as Van Diemen's Land.) Scott the bibliomaniac would certainly have been attracted by this, and Field's facetious comments have proved to be prophetic. The editor of the 1966 facsimile reprint of the Howe booklet knew of only three copies: in the Bodleian, the British Library, and the National Library of Australia (Craig [vii]). The one sent by Macquarie is still part of Scott's library at Abbotsford (*Catalogue* 127) and would seem to be the fourth known copy and probably one of the most valuable books in the library.

However I would suggest there was another interest for Scott in the book. For one thing he would have found the language used to describe the activities of the bushrangers very familiar. Take this passage:

> They [the bushrangers] were a heavy drawback upon the industry of young colony; and settlers were fain to pay them black-mail as a composition for escape from worse plunder. It was more than conjectured in Van Diemen's Land that these freebooters could not have maintained themselves so long, had they not found abettors, concealers, and receivers of their spoils. They would *lift* a flock of sheep from one farmer and turn it into the pasture of another, marking the animals as his. (Field 82)

It was Scott himself, in *Waverley* and later *Rob Roy*, who had made the terms *black-mail* and *lift* meaning 'to steal animals in a raid' very familiar to English readers (although *lift* is applied here to sheep, rather than cattle in the distinctive Scottish usage). The language, if nothing else, would have made immediately linked these antipodean outlaws in Scott's mind with the Scottish outlaws about whom he had written so much. Another familiar term is *banditti* which is applied to freebooting Highlanders in *Waverley* (99) and *Rob Roy* (246) and which Scott was to apply, as I have already pointed out, to those in *Bizarro*, with more obvious appropriateness.

However I would suggest that there was another source of interest for him and one which relates more closely to the subject of this paper. Even the brief account given by Field of Howe's 'six years of plunder and cruelty', the bushranger emerges as violent and cruel. This, for example, is how he is characterised:

> Howe was without a spark of even the honour of an outlaw; he betrayed his colleagues upon surrendering himself to government, and he fired upon the native girl, his companion, when she became an impediment to his flight. He was reduced at last to abandonment, even by his own gang; and 100 guineas, and (if a convict should take him) a free pardon and a passage to England, were set upon his head. He was now a wretched, conscience-haunted solitary, hiding in dingles, and only tracked by the sagacity of the native girl, to whom he had behaved so ungratefully, and who was now employed by the police to revenge his cruelty to her. (Field 72)

Here we find a similar motif to that which Scott had particularly picked out from the stories surrounding Francesco Moscato – betrayal by his wife after an act of cruelty and ingratitude towards her. Indeed, Scott's *Bizarro* provides further suggestive evidence of his fascination with this particular element of the Moscato story. Although he did not get as far as Bizarro's death in the incomplete novella, Scott had already set up circumstances favourable to such a conclusion. Before he gave up writing he had introduced an abused woman destined to be Bizarro's wife and had endowed her with the skill in the use of firearms necessary for her to kill her husband in revenge like her historical model. It seems reasonable to assume that his incomplete novella was heading towards this violent conclusion.

When it finally arrived Macquarie's gift would have proved as germane to his interests as Field's review had suggested it might be. For instance, he would have found more information about how the bushrangers interacted with the local community:

> The property taken from individuals by this lawless gang must ... have been immense; and it is not to be conceived how it was appropriated but by their having confederates in society, though unsuspected, who not only purchased their booty, but were channels of information as to the passing events in which they were interested: and, indeed, we may safely ascribe the long period in which they eluded every exertion made to capture them to this secret support. (*Michael Howe* 14)

Just how familiar Scott was with such situations is made clear years later in *Bizarro* where he relates a very similar situation to events in earlier Scottish history with which he had long been very familiar:

> Their existence and occasional peculation were a great evil to the peaceful inhabitants, the lowest of whom, however, learned, as is usually the case with those in their situation, to indemnify themselves by *packing and peeling*, as it is called in the old Scottish Statutes, or developing that sort of connexion between guilt and innocence which cannot subsist without the latter becoming sullied by the communication. Those who were thus the hosts, unwilling hosts perhaps, of these robbers became in this manner glad to pay them protection money in proportion to their property, which on that condition their guests spared. Or they observed heedfully the secrets of their route, which otherwise could hardly be easily concealed from them. Or they bought the plunder which the brigands collected in the district, rendering their crimes beneficial and availing to them. (*Bizarro* 166)

He would also have found familiar language such as he had himself used, including the constant application of the term *banditti* to Howe and his gang (*Michael Howe* 10, 13, 14, 30).

More importantly for the discussion here, the book sent by Macquarie also portrays Howe as an extremely violent and savage man. Much of the commentary in *Michael Howe* is rather general, such as comments about how he and his band practised 'every wanton atrocity' (14) or the claim that he was 'the most hardened and sanguinary' (30) of his band. When we are told that the last six years of his life comprised 'a series of crimes committed with the coolest indifference' we might well recall Moscato's cold-blooded callousness and cruelty. On the whole the writer avoids specific stories but one of the few certainly suggests a lesser Moscato – in an appendix we read how

> On a subsequent occasion, at a creek on Salt-pan Plains, Bowles having sportively discharged a pistol over Howe's head, the latter in a wanton and cruel manner tied Bowles, hands and feet, and then coolly shot him dead. (35)

In short, Howe performs acts of the same 'cold-blooded atrocity dextrously contrived' (*Bizarro* 167) as Scott himself attributed to the life of his fictional Domenichino, themselves suggested to him by the real-life Moscato. There is, moreover, no reason to believe that Scott found Howe any less fascinating than Moscato.

What then are we to make of this apparent interest in extreme violence on Scott's part? As I have already noted, Scott's novels and poetry seem to avoid such excessive violence. Where we find violence it is usually what one might call necessary violence in the sense that there is no gratuitous indulgence of extra violence beyond what is needed to achieve the perpetrator's purpose. Morris's death is horrible but there is no additional violence beyond what is needed to kill him. So too for Oliver Proudfute in *The Fair Maid of Perth*. I have suggested elsewhere that Scott was more willing to portray violence when freed from the continual supervision of Ballantyne, Cadell, and Lockhart who acted as the guardians of the sensibilities of his audience. It was Ballantyne, after all, who forced him to resuscitate Athelstone in *Ivanhoe* after Scott had originally had him dying with his head cloven in two (Tulloch 36–38). The absence of his habitual censors might account for his willingness to portray the mutilation of the corpse of Antonio in *Bizarro* but it still does not explain why Scott wanted to present this scene. I would suggest that, like many people, Scott felt a fascinated interest in extreme violence. But if this is so, why did he not portray it more often? I have already suggested one explanation – censorship or self-censorship for the sake of his audience – and I believe it is a valid one.

However *Bizarro* also suggests a second, rather different explanation. The relevant passage is rather garbled in Scott's manuscript but the general sense is clear. I will quote it as my fellow editors and I have reconstructed it. Scott first explains that his hero gained the name of il Bizarro

> not only characterising him for the shrewdness and address by which this bravo's enterprizes were marked, but the audacity and bravery, as well as the daring inhumanity, with which they were hatched and conducted to their terrible determination. (167)

He then goes on to say, in words I have already partly quoted, that

> the reputation which this man had formed to himself, frightful as it was for the crimes he had committed with a sort of stoicism unnaturally and unnecessarily hideous, had only to be recounted to excite a sense of cold-blooded atrocity dextrously contrived. (167; reading 'stoicism' from the manuscript for 'scheme')

Having thus acknowledged the extreme and unnecessary violence of Domenichino, Scott then adds a revealing comment:

> However the scenery of his exploits is not indifferent, nor are the incidents themselves, to the lovers of the wonderful and romantic, to which we are compelled to add the vulgar appetite for the horrible and the atrocious. (167)

As I read this 'lovers of the wonderful and romantic' are the body of respectable readers who had read and enjoyed Scott's work and given him his fame. But he is also 'compelled', to use his word, to recognise that the story appealed to another taste as well, 'the vulgar appetite for the horrible and the atrocious'. Stories of outlaws of the past could be reworked to give prominence to 'the wonderful and the romantic' but there was an immediacy about stories of contemporary outlaws which pushed 'the horrible and the atrocious' to the fore. In reworking the life of his contemporary Moscato Scott was, I would argue, 'compelled' to recognise his own participation in 'the vulgar appetite for the horrible and the atrocious'. For someone who had spent so much of his life drawing a careful line between the 'polite' and the 'vulgar' and aligning himself and his writing with the polite, it must have been an uncomfortable revelation.

We do not know directly how Scott reacted to the story of Michael Howe. As far as I can discover he did not write to Macquarie about it, he did not mention it in other letters, and he did not refer to it in his journal. Nor did he plan to write a story based on it. He met Barron Field in Edinburgh in 1827 but there is nothing to suggest they discussed Howe. Yet the example of his reaction to Moscato would suggest that he might have discovered in regard to Howe as well that he had a certain rather perturbing interest in 'the horrible and the atrocious'. If this is so, is it too much to suggest that he felt a certain shame in sharing this 'vulgar appetite' and that this shameful consciousness prevented him from displaying extreme violence in his novels except where it could be safely compartmentalised as being of purely historical interest? Thus instances of extreme violence, such as the torture of the Abbot of Crossraguel, were cited in the notes to the 'Magnum' collected Waverley Novels (in this case in the notes to *Ivanhoe*), but only the threat of violence or, at most, relatively mild violence could generally find its way into the novels themselves. However in Italy, far from his habitual censors and perhaps relaxing a little in his self-censorship, he allowed his latent interest in this topic to surface and permitted extreme, unnecessary and, significantly, *contemporary* violence to invade his fictional world.

Texts cited

Catalogue of the Library at Abbotsford. Edinburgh: [privately printed], 1838.

Craig, C. Introduction. *Michael Howe, The Last and Worst of the Bush Rangers of Van Diemen's Land: A Facsimile Reproduction*. Hobart: Platypus, 1966, [vi–vii]

Macquarie, Lachlan. Letter to Walter Scott, 21 November 1821. National Library of Scotland, MS 3893, ff. 165–66.

Michael Howe, the Last and Worst of the Bush Rangers of Van Diemen's Land. Hobart Town: [printed by Andrew Bent], 1818.

Prestera, Vincenzo. 'Dettaglio del famoso Francesco Muscato Bizzarro brigante della provincia di Calabria formato dal Quartier Mastro della Legione Sig. Vincenzo Prestera'. Ilario Principe, *L'Ultima Plebe: contributi per la storia del brigantaggio calabrese*. Chiaravelle Centrale: Effe Emme, 1977. 173–81

Field, Barron. Rev. of *Michael Howe, the Last and Worst of the Bush Rangers of Van Diemen's Land*. *Quarterly Review*, 12 (1820): 73–83.

Lockhart, J.G. *Memoirs of the Life of Sir Walter Scott, Bart.* 7 vols. Edinburgh: Robert Cadell, 1837–38.

Quarterly Review Archive www.rc.umd.edu/reference/qr/index/45.html

Scott, Walter. *Bizarro*. *The Siege of Malta* and *Bizarro*. Ed. J.H. Alexander, Judy King, and Graham Tulloch. Edinburgh: Edinburgh UP, 2008.

Scott, Walter. *The Journal of Sir Walter Scott*. Ed. W.E.K. Anderson. Oxford: Clarendon Press, 1972.

Scott, Walter. *Rob Roy*. Ed. David Hewitt. Edinburgh: Edinburgh UP, 2008.

Scott, Walter. *Waverley*. Ed. P.D. Garside. Edinburgh: Edinburgh UP, 2007.

Sticchini, [?]. Letter to Walter Scott, 24 April 1832. National Library of Scotland, MS 5317, f. 232.

Tulloch, Graham. 'Writing "by Advice": *Ivanhoe* and *The Three Perils of Man*.' *Studies in Hogg and His World* 15 (2004): 32–52.

Valente, Angela. *Gioacchino Murat e l'Italia meridionale*. New ed. Turin: Einaudi, 1965.

For Syd

TREVOR FENNELL
FLINDERS UNIVERSITY

1

A Reader-cum-Writer, Syd Harrex,
Said, mulling an opus of Garrick's:
'For the best comprehension
Of the fellow's intention
I need numerous Pernods and araks.'

2

Syd Harrex is an amphibrach.
He thinks that Illing sounds like Bach,
And, Thomas-hints ignoring,
He adamantly still reserves
For Twyfords his outpouring.

Saying it with Flowers: A Marriage Made in Hobart

SUSAN HOSKING
UNIVERSITY OF ADELAIDE

Gardens always mean something else,
man absolutely uses one thing to say another.
Robert Harbison, *Eccentric Spaces*, 1977

Mary Ann Meredith (1795–1843) was the second wife of George Meredith (1778–1856), one of the most prominent free settlers in Tasmania. Much is known about George's public life, but his private life, including his marriage to Mary Ann, is more of a mystery. The extensive Meredith Family Papers, in the Tasmanian Archive and Heritage Office, provide little insight into Mary Ann, the person. However, Family Papers held in the University of Tasmania Library, including some private letters, invite speculation about Mary Ann's role as a colonial wife. Such speculation is further fired by gaps in official records and correspondence files, which can be taken as evidence that Mary Ann, unlike her husband, was not the kind of woman who would be well received in Hobart. Furthermore, it seems that her 'gentleman' husband was all too conscious of the detrimental effect her lack of breeding might have on his own reputation. In hindsight, it is tempting to describe George, in the context of his colonial marriage, as 'a very unattractive man'. That is not what Mary Ann thought, at least to begin with. Towards the end of her life as Mrs Meredith, Mary Ann's silence makes it impossible to know the extent of changes in her emotions. Nevertheless, some of her few surviving letters to her husband, and even more fascinating letters from George, in Hobart, to his wife, in distant Swansea, imply disillusionment and serve to critique conventions of behaviour, in relation to gender and, more particularly, class in colonial Hobart.

George was the youngest of four sons of John Meredith, an eminent barrister and solicitor in Birmingham, whose family claimed to belong to a long line of princely ancestors in South Wales (Edwin Meredith, unpublished typescript). His father died when George was eleven, from sleeping in a damp bed, it was said, while on circuit. At the age of eighteen, George received a commission in the navy, as a second lieutenant, and served in the West Indies and later in America, the Mediterranean and Egypt. In 1805 he met, ran away with and married Miss Sarah Hicks, the seventeen-year old daughter of Colonel Hicks. She had a property next to that of Lord Craven in Berkshire, but her substantial dowry of about £5,000 was misappropriated by lawyers. George, having retired as a first lieutenant on half-pay from the Marine Corps of the Royal Navy, took up farming – in Berkshire, then in Wales. He had already decided to emigrate to Australia when on February 6th 1820 Sarah, aged 31, inconveniently died, leaving five children, including a baby.

By October of the same year, George, aged forty-four, was married again, to Miss Mary Evans, aged twenty-five, if the records are correct. She has been described, by other members of the Meredith family, and subsequently by David Hodgson in the *Australian Dictionary of Biography* entry on George Meredith, as a governess, but George's private letters to Mary Ann imply that, at least initially, she did not enjoy this status and was not trained. She had helped to look after the children while Sarah was sick – more to the point, dying – after the birth of her last child. George's later letters to Mary Ann suggest that George was paying Mary Ann a great deal of attention while he was still married to Sarah.

It is clear from George's letters that his relatives did not approve of his second marriage, and it is unlikely that George would have married beneath him had he not already decided to leave England for Van Diemen's Land. As it was, he sailed away without having to change his plans, with minimum disruption to the family structure and a new wife who knew how to work hard and, again this is clear from George's letters, enjoy herself and pleasure her man. There were also financial incentives. George's experience of farming entitled him to a substantial grant of land (maximum 2,000 acres) for £200 – a sum he borrowed from an actor friend.

The family arrived in Hobart in March, 1821. George took 'a small unfurnished cottage' for his family, about three miles out of town, where he left them while he explored the east coast, looking for land. Six months later, George had chosen his acreage and a year after their arrival in Tasmania he moved his family to Greater Swan Port, one hundred and twenty miles from Hobart up the eastern coast, with four servants and sixteen members of the Amos families (who proved useful to him in a deceitful arrangement to acquire more land from the government than he was entitled to – in fact, he ended up with 50,000 acres).

Initially Mary Ann lived on the land grant at Swan Port in a turf hut with George's five children, their first baby, Henry, and their second baby John. Five years later, in 1827, they moved into a wattle and daub hut called Belmont, where their daughter Maria was born. George and Mary Ann's fourth child, Edwin, was also born in 1827. There were three more girls: Clara, Fanny and Rosina. Mary Ann looked after twelve children in the course of her life.

By 1830 George had moved his now substantial family into Cambria House, designed by himself and built by a convict stonemason, known as 'Old Bull'. Around the 25-roomed stone and brick house a beautiful garden was established. In *My Home in Tasmania*, the writer, artist and conservationist Louisa Anne Meredith (1812–1895), who married George's second son Charles, waxes lyrical about the garden, its fine orchard, grassy walks and in particular, one 'bowery path' with its rustic bench shaded by English elders, their fragrant cream blossoms mingling with the native wattles. She also admired the thickets of hazel bushes and the cultivated English and Cape flowers, interspersed with flowering indigenous shrubs.

Edwin Meredith writes in his unpublished memoirs that the trees, hedges and orchard of Cambria House were being planted in the years when the house was being built, and that he and his mother, with a gardener, marked out the flower and vegetable gardens. There were, of course, always convicts to do the hard physical work in establishing a gentleman's garden. Mary Ann was clearly extraordinarily competent at managing not only the Meredith children and household, but also the developing Cambria, a gentleman's estate. George relied on her to keep track of and maintain many of his business interests. Unlike the argumentative George, Mary Ann made friends easily, giving away rabbits that were bred in a special enclosure at Cambria. No doubt she also received and exchanged cuttings, bulbs and seedlings, as was common practice amongst colonial women gardeners.

During their time of settlement on the property at Greater Swan Port, just to the north of present-day Swansea, George was often away, establishing the family sealing and bay whaling enterprises, negotiating with the colonial administration to win contracts to supply convict stations, or engaged in litigation when his wishes were thwarted. Before moving to Cambria, when George was away and while Mary Ann was looking after the family in the turf hut, a notorious bushranger named Matthew Brady, one of 130 known armed bushrangers in 1825, attacked the Meredith hut, tied up the servants, kept them under armed guard, and demanded that Mary Ann Meredith and her daughters feed and wait upon them. From a distance, George was aware at the time of 'desperate banditti', as he called them, ranging the district. The following year he warned Mary Ann, still from a distance of 120 miles away in comfortable accommodation in Hobart, not to 'go about without one of the Girls with you & then not to any Distance unprotected'. The family kept dogs, probably trained to drive away the 'savages', as Edwin described the local Indigenous people, who had already killed one of the workmen and thrown lighted spears into the thatched roof.

When he was establishing Cambria as the key property of the Swansea district, George made bitter enemies. The acreage he chose was already settled. The local Indigenous people of course did not register in the colonial mentality as occupants, but settlers did, and George turfed them out with no sympathy. Appeals were made to Governor Sorell; family feuds developed as people in the district took sides and ill feeling prevailed for many years (*Pioneers of the East Coast*, Stieglitz, 31). George even quarrelled with his own son, George Junior, over their sealing and bay whaling activities and over his egalitarian associations with his assigned convicts. George Junior then stole a family whaleboat and left Van Diemen's Land for Kangaroo Island with a Bruny Island woman called Maggerlede, Trukinnini's sister. George Senior would not allow his first-born son's name to be mentioned thereafter.

By the time she was thirty-five, Mary Ann had a large brood of children to look after and a 'large, well-built, cheerful-looking house, with ... accompanying signs of substantial comfort' including 'extensive gardens' (Louisa Anne Meredith, 89). This signalled domestic bliss, in the way that a gentleman's home and garden should, but all was not as it seemed. By the early 1830s, George Meredith's trips to Hobart involved longer and longer stays, and he was even absent for the family celebrations that were so important to Mary Ann: birthdays, anniversaries and Christmases.

What remains to tantalise us about this marriage is some curious correspondence between Mary Ann and George, written between 1825 and 1831. This has already been noted by Sharon Morgan, in an article on the 'The Role of the Colonial Wife' published in 1989. Morgan observes the hollowness of Meredith's excuses to his wife, concluding that he was ashamed of her: as he surely was. Only thirteen of Mary Ann's letters have survived. In all probability George destroyed most of them. George's many carefully saved letters imply that his wife wrote at least as regularly as he did.

In his letters to Mary Ann George attempts to maintain the intimacy of what had clearly been a robust sexual relationship, and, at a distance, to satisfy his second wife, who was also conveniently his farm manager, secretary, clerk, business manager and carer of his many children. George returns in his letters again and again to the day he 'deflowered' Mary Ann, praising her youthful beauty, attempting to appease her frequently implied concern that she might no longer be attractive to him by assuring her of his fidelity.

> That you are not exactly what you were at seventeen – I admit – and although my wishes as well as your own would again restore you to all the Virgin Bloom & loveliness of that Day – still – ... I have no ambition beyond that of your husband ... you *were* [my italics] perfect in his Eyes. (24 April 1825)

As for 'sweet seventeen', that was Sarah's age when he ran away with her.

Mary Ann was a loyal wife and devoted mother; that seems to have been enough for her, at least for the first seven or eight years. She clearly attempted to do whatever George thought best, to please him, even if she didn't see why.

> I have bathed both myself and my beautiful tresses as you are pleased to call them in the sea but have not derived the least benefit from it in any way as to those little swellings I think you are good enough to interest yourself about, nothing will ever remove them in my opinion soon [as] if I was to grow thin (March [?] 1827)

George worried about Mary Ann's handwriting because others would see it on the letters she addressed to him in Hobart. Mary Ann practised, as instructed by George, and with time her writing shows some improvement. But it is never good enough for George, and his admonitions become stronger and stronger.

> bethink yourself of the additional pleasure which you have the power to convey to me by always preserving the same neatness & good style ... make your letters to me distinguishable for the penmanship of the superscription – indeed – my love I am more anxious about these things than you seem to be aware of. (25 July 1827)

A couple of years later he is still nagging, from Hobart:

> I must remind you that you still are too careless in writing your letters – in proof of which are several Grammatical errors in the letter I saw last night. Do I pray you my Dear Girl not only write neatly but examine & correct before sending your letters. (2nd October 1829)

In less than a month he is at it again:

> One single misspelt word in the letter of a lady or a Gentleman excites remarks and frequently lead to enquiries of who & what the party have been – their ... education & former situation in life. **Need I say more.** [underlined twice] (14th Nov. 1829)

While clearly George relied on Mary Ann to take care not only of the children and household, but also of business on the land holding, and even some of the business relating to George's sealing and bay whaling interests, he knew that this was inappropriate for a lady. In 1827 he promises that in the not too distant future she will be relieved from farm matters and occupations unbefitting a proper lady (23 July 1827).

Particularly fascinating in the letters is the way in which George involves his wife in what might be described as genteel pornography – something he justifies to Mary Ann as the means of cementing their marriage vows. George and Mary Ann, evidently on George's instigation and continued insistence, titillate each other with allusions to intercourse couched in the language and symbolism of flowers and gardening. On the one hand, this is in keeping with 'the language of refined and modest courtship'. As the Melbourne publisher and bookseller E.W. Cole (1832–1918), of Coles Funny Picture Books fame, wrote in the nineteenth century: 'Millions have conveyed a message by presenting a flower that they dare not have uttered in their mother tongue' (*Coles Funny Picture Book* No. 1, 146).

As a gentleman, George would have been aware of such courtship language: cape jasmine for 'transport of joy'; tuberose for 'dangerous pleasures'; wisteria saying 'I cling to you'; irises declaring 'I burn', and so forth. But George and Mary Ann were way past courtship and Mary Ann was not really a lady. It seems that in order to keep Mary Ann literally in her place, on the farm, where she was indispensable, George attempted to satisfy her in a way that was familiar to him, drawing upon pornographic stories that he may well have become familiar with during his days in the navy, sailing with American officers and in the West Indies.

B.R. Burg has written interestingly on officers, gentlemen and 'man-talk' in the American Navy in the nineteenth century. Burg draws attention to the discrepancy between the prescribed behaviour of the gentlemen officers at public functions and social and cultural gatherings, and the realities of life at sea. In public, officers 'laboured to emulate a polished and meticulously cultivated ideal of well-educated, cultured, and self-restrained ... manliness' (2). The cardinal rule for naval gentlemen was that 'no man spoke of politics, religion, or women'. But on board ship, things were different. At least one passionate diarist, Philip C. Van Buskirk, compiled an extensive record of his service in the American navy, when his mother enlisted him as a marine drummer boy. This was a few decades after George Meredith served in the navy, but Van Buskirk's volumes of transcribed conversations provide copious evidence that riotous and unfettered sexual escapes were the favourite topic of the wardroom. Van Buskirk complained:

> '[T]heir talk always runs upon trifles – drinking, eating, whoring, and 'pleasure' generally, are the never-ending themes ... they never tire of recounting their exploits.' (10–11) 'The conversation ... runs continually in the same direction ... We all know [of these officers'] amours. They are recounted not once but daily, joked upon nor seldom but hourly.' (12)

As Burg observes, the naval officers' 'pervasive sexual chatter' and 'fascination with pornography could easily be characterised as gross hypocrisy, but the disjunction between the proffered gentlemanly ideals and the profligate character of American officers' (39) at sea is of course more complex. Nevertheless, the point is that a gentleman would not subject his lady mother, lady aunt, lady sister, lady wife, sweetheart, female lady friends, or daughters to such stories. That is not to say that ladies and gentlemen in significant relationships could not share an erotic life. But while George Meredith was chastising Mary Ann for her lack of ladies' accomplishments, he continued to treat her in private as he would never have treated a lady. Maintaining some kind of intimacy with his second wife was crucial to George's business interests. He seems to have assumed that the behind-the-scenes pornography of the wardroom, while inappropriate for well-bred women, would be good enough for Mary Ann. The couple might have been soul-mates, as descendents of the Meredith family like to maintain. However, it is difficult to escape our current understanding of pornography as taking 'sexuality, a deep fact about our lives, and enlist[ing] it – as idea, identity, desire and practice – in support of subordination'. As Joshua Cohen insists:

> Pornography is not a treatise that justifies subordination, but a device that makes it seem right, look natural, feel good. By producing a psychocultural setting that makes us experience sexism as irresistible, it closes off all avenues of exit from subordination. (269)

George required Mary Ann to participate in the writing of 'scenes', which he called garden experiences. There are, or were, since they were destroyed with most of Mary Ann's letters, stories by Mary Ann about Maria and the Captain, Maria and the Baron, and the Noble Baron and the fair Maria. George refers to Maria's versions of the stories critically, mostly because they are not detailed enough, too detailed in the wrong way, not varied enough or not stimulating enough. He urges her to try harder: 'let your fancy dwell on new methods of adding to the happiness of that meeting' (9th April, 1829).

By far the most common story, 'scene', 'dream' or fantasy that the couple share is the 'garden ramble' which taps the English literary erotic symbolism of flowers, though for all his criticism of Mary Ann, George reveals a distinct lack of imagination: 'Why do I so notice and attend to your flowers and little shrubs so fondly – why are the former pressed to my bosom and lips – the latter so often by my hand' (6 April 1829). Prosaically, while he refers to the erotic fragrance of his wife's 'flowers', he constantly reminds Mary Ann that she must take time 'for a hasty watering of the flowers and shrubs & the arrangement of the Bower' (14th Nov. 1829) before he visits the Garden.

Harmless fantasies, in themselves, the fact nevertheless remains that the 'garden rambles' served George's needs, rather than Mary Ann's. Her desire was to be physically with her husband; while she obviously tried to please him with her letters, she didn't see the point of games or stories when what she really wanted was the real thing. George constantly denied Mary Ann's requests to be with him in Hobart. The accommodation wasn't suitable. The ladies of Hobart might discover her humble origins. They couldn't both be away from Cambria at the same time. By July 1827, Mary Ann is obviously giving up hope that she will ever be invited to share George's company in Hobart. By early 1829, she has told George that he is not missed. George is surprised.

> You say that I have not been once wanted in the Garden since my departure – surely my dear M. you might have added that I had at least been wished for ... instead of being told that I was not wanted – I might rather have expected to hear that could you have caught me unexpectedly there some morning or evening you would have made me your prisoner for (say how many) hours that would have so engaged my time – so agreeably varied the scene & given that enchantment to the whole that if I regretted any thing – it should have been my release from bondage. (6 April 1929)

Curiously, it is when Mary Ann seems to be losing interest that George plays the gardener with most vitality and the 'scenes' become most urgent.

> I recommend Deep Planting which you tell me you had to approve when you were first initiated into this interesting science & yet I think you have occasionally scolded me for planting too deep. However ladies will sometimes change their mind and as you have not as much experience as myself – are both younger & more active and may probably frequently feel inclined for a ramble when I do not think of proposing it I believe I had better at once get you to assume the entire management of the Garden and I will act under your directions – as far as circumstances will permit ... (14th Nov. 1829)

It is possible that George's time in the West Indies exposed him to the Creole sensibility that enjoyed a very relaxed attitude to the pleasures of sex: one of the few pleasures, and, as the contemporary Haitian poet Rene Depestre suggests, perhaps the only form of freedom allowed to slaves on colonial plantations. Reflecting on his erotic heritage, Depestre writes: 'the woman achieves fulfilment in a paradise garden, clasped in the arms of the enchanter, a gardener whose spade thrusts and turns passionately in the innermost parts of her adorable body' (*UNESCO Courier*, April 1993). In this tradition the woman is conceived as a garden, to be brought to fulfilment from bare earth that must first be dug and planted. As Depestre explains it, there is 'a marvellous freedom in the employment of the intimate parts involved in bringing' lovemaking to its 'glorious' conclusion. In stories and poetry from this tradition, the act of love-making is described lyrically, in 'dream-like terms', using garden imagery, focussed on mutual pleasure, with any thought of sin securely locked away. George Meredith may well have read or heard crude versions of such stories recounted by naval cronies, but judging by Burg's work on the taste for pornography amongst naval officers at sea, the lyricism of the poetic tradition would have been the least of their interest.

The scenes in George's letters are often conceived as dreams. As the gardener he arrives with plants and seeds. He asks that his partner direct his attention to the appropriate bushes and buds. He insists on mutual pleasure as they undertake their garden rambles. But in the end, George Meredith is no poet. In the end, Mary Ann is still at home, pretty much alone, managing George's family and his estate. In a letter to Mary Ann dated 28 April 1832, George refers to 'the silence upon what used to form not the least interesting portion of your correspondence'. He remembers the time when 'midst ... more pressing farm matters you would have found space for a few Garden references if only to remind me that my <u>favourite flowers</u> were 'wasting their sweetness on the desert air''.

By 1839, George and Mary Ann's daughters, Fanny and Clara, were at boarding school in Hobart, and, by Hobart standards, behaving badly. Charlotte Betts, perhaps as friend or at least as a well-meaning acquaintance with a critical awareness of the particulars of snobbery in Hobart town, wrote to warn Mary Ann that she must tell her girls to be 'most circumspect in their manners'. Children raised in the country, Mrs Betts suggests, do not have 'the restraint of the Town's People' (26 September, 1839). In the same letter, Mrs Betts observes: 'the greatest hypocrites gain the day in this world'. There is nothing in the fragments of Mary Ann's writing to suggest that she was inclined to reflect upon life's ironies. Nor is there any overt criticism of Mr Meredith, who had judged her, his own wife, unsuitable for Hobart society. We can only speculate on what she felt in her mid-forties, as her nest at Cambria emptied and she headed towards the end of her not-so-long life. She seems to have gone very, very quiet.

Texts cited

Burg, B.R. *An American Seafarer in the Age of Sale. The Erotic Diaries of Philip C. Van Buskirk, 1851–1870.* Yale University Press, New Haven, 1994.

Cohen, Joshua. 'Freedom, Equality, Pornography' in *Prostitution and Pornography: Philosophical Debate About the Sex Industry*, edited by Jessica Spencer, Stanford: Stanford University Press, 2006, 269.

Cole, E.W. *Coles Funny Picture Book* No. 1, 146.

Depestre, Rene. 'The Enchanted garden – Caribbean erotic culture', UNESCO Courier, April, 1993 <http://findarticles.com/p/articles/mi_m1310/is_1993_April/ai_14332557> downloaded November 29, 2007.

Hodgson, David. 'Meredith, George (1777–1856)'. *Australian Dictionary of Biography.*

Meredith Family. [Papers] Tasmanian Archive and Heritage Office. NG123.

Meredith Family Papers. University of Tasmania. G.4/A.

Meredith, Edwin. Untitled Typescript ['Memoir of George Meredith'], 1897. State Library of Tasmania, 920 MER.

Meredith, Louisa Anne (Mrs Charles Meredith). *My Home in Tasmania, During a Residence of Nine Years.* Facsimile Edition, Glamorgan Spring Bay Historical Society, Swansea, Tasmania, 2003 (London: John Murray, 1852).

Morgan, Sharon. 'George and Mary Meredith: The Role of the Colonial Wife'. *Tasmanian Historical Research Association. Papers and Proceedings.* 36, 3 (September 1989), 125–129.

Stieglitz, Karl von. *Pioneers of the East Coast from 1642* (Launceston, 1955).

A Sort of Sequence for Syd

PAUL SHARRAD
UNIVERSITY OF WOLLONGONG

Dhvanyaloka

On a gentle rise at the edge of town,
the house, like a station homestead, fences off
wandering cows in a square of wind-whispered
eucalypts. Each morning the young widow
waves puja fire beneath them then scooters to school.
The old man squats on lounge-room concrete
polished by the years. He's stuffing envelopes
with learning, his family gluing flaps,
writing addresses – a cottage industry
with global reach. Quiet rigour, ideals of
Anandavardhana and Leavis kept
bounds and opened first to you and later me
worlds of difference, familiar offerings,
a vision of truth behind mere seeing.

Delhi

Jantar Mantar's a sonnet in stone: a
Calculated frenzy, grid, filigree
Of numbers, one set echoing another,
All tracking avatars: the ziggurat,
Stonehenge, a stick in the sand. You must know
All there is to know to build this system,
That then will make the magic from which fire
Stairways catch stars, stone cauldrons offer up
A map of what you knew and need to know.
Such finesse, that whole elegance of form
Contains nothing of complete symmetry!
(Tourist plaques a new critical lesson:
unhelpful obvious paraphrase leaves mystery;
the thing itself fires imagination.)

Doxos

Your fiery insistence on retaining
'New Literatures in English' in face of
postcolonial politics was surprising,
but cookie-cutter applications of
hybridity, the subaltern, Said
and co. have shown how specificities
of the literary are leached away
in the thesis mills, the poet's words
'placed under erasure', a pretext to
the critic's cleverness. Nothing new or
even English there; the drummer's pitch,
quaver of the muezzin, the conch's blast,
carnival's beat, these are the offerings
we must heed or there is no art, just words.

Salute

Before the fire of Kurukshetra, there's
An offering, and all troops fight better fed.
For us, you were yourself the offering,
And we were fed by all those hosts you mustered:
On page, in person, worlds came to our table,
Till lunchtime made a legend in the world.
Since then, we tend our own fires, scrape rations
To feed the new recruits, and hold a line
That moves through half a world at least, inspired
Still by what your life and writings teach:
Pythagoras and Hopkins, like the old
Masters and Desani, were never wrong:
The fire is the offering, we are offerings
To the fire. The burning is our song.

Kenneth Slessor's 'Other Front'

JULIAN CROFT
UNIVERSITY OF NEW ENGLAND

Kenneth Slesssor's first published poem at the age of 16 was in the *Bulletin* ('Goin'', 19 July 1917) and was a tribute to a dying Australian soldier after the Anzac landings. For the sixteen year-old, no doubt reflecting C.E.W. Bean's influence, the individual death and the wider military defeat are redeemed by the prospect of joining his mates in death and glory on another front, and as he leaves this world the soldier imagines the he hears the surf at Manly and the sights of Sydney Harbour. Slessor finished school as the Armistice was signed, but not before publishing two more poems on the war – 'France – 1918' and 'Jerusalem Set Free' – both celebrating the Anzac tradition and seeing purpose and sense in those years of awful conflict.

In 1942, just across the Mediterranean from Gallipoli, Slessor experienced a personal and professional crisis and out of it wrote a poem on one of the most significant battles of the Second World War. He was to claim it in 1952 as his last poem (it wasn't, but he must have meant it was his last significant poem), saying that he had written nothing substantial after it and after his wife's death in 1945. I have written elsewhere on why Noela's death and Slessor's resultant poetic silence (he wrote no more poetry after he turned 46) should not be read as a counsel of despair, in fact quite the reverse (Croft, 198–211). My argument was based on a reading of absence and presence in his poetry, in which his major emotional and intellectual stimulus came from the notion of absence. 'Beach Burial' is a curious combination of presence and absence, of inscription and erasure, a product of Slessor's experiences as a war correspondent, and the culmination of his poetic career. It ends with a gesture towards presence and purpose is its references to another front, but just what the front might be is the subject of this paper.

To return to 1942 and the genesis of the poem 'Beach Burial'. In 1940 Slessor was offered the position C.E.W. Bean had so productively filled in the First World War: that of Official War Correspondent to the Australian forces, with the expectation that at the end of the War he might write part of the official war history. Having just published his great elegiac summary of the vacuum and pointlessness of life in the 1930s, 'Five Bells', and after having been through domestic and professional trials, this appointment must have seemed like a heroic challenge and one which he hoped to fill with commitment and purpose. He had few doubts (and many others shared his conviction) about the validity of the cause the second AIF was embarking on, nor of the ability of the Australian soldier to meet the trials ahead. For once life must have seemed to have a meaning, and to be more than the purposeless vacuum of 'Five Bells' and the nihilism of peace time.

Slessor spent 1942 in the Middle East. He had been there from early 1941 and he had covered the disastrous campaign in Greece and Crete, and while he celebrated the courage and stoicism of the ordinary Australian soldier, he was beginning to realise the deficiencies in Allied leadership, both Australian and British. His job as Official War Correspondent was complicated by the arrival in October 1941 of his wife Noela from England where she had followed him in 1940. Slessor had been actively involved in writing despatches about the campaign against the Vichy French in Lebanon and it was during this time that some of the first images (and in fact the symbolic argument) of 'Beach Burial' occurred in his writing.

Returning from Beirut to Cairo by car in July 1941 he stopped not far from the Litani River at some Australian battle graves (Semmler, 262–3). Two of them by striking co-incidence shared the same surname 'La France', two soldiers both killed on the same day and both from South Australia. Without proof, Slessor was reluctant to say they were brothers, and changed the text of his despatch to say they were 'comrades'. The paragraph describing the brothers' graves (it seems hard to believe they were not) is the first evidence we have of the genesis of 'Beach Burial':

> The crosses were the simple sides of packing cases nailed at right angles and the inscription, written with careful clumsiness in indelible pencil, had been smeared violet by the rain. The two comrades lay side by side facing the white beach and the blue sea, so piercing blue that it might have been stolen from their South Australian coast. (Semmler, 262)

He returned to the site four months later to find the brothers now located in a War Graves Commission cemetery, still side-by-side, but now in properly marked graves with permanent inscriptions. Significantly for the genesis of the poem, they were surrounded by fifteen other graves with the simple inscription 'unknown soldier'. Here in these two scenes we have the dialectic of the poem: transience and permanence, erasure and inscription, naming and being. It was an allegory of the war and Slessor's role in it as Official War Correspondent (naming, inscribing, making permanent), which was to haunt his imagination during the following year.

By the end of 1941 Noela had joined Slessor in Cairo as the war in the Middle East ebbed and flowed along the North African littoral until it finally reached a crisis with the arrival of Rommel at El Alamein (only 120 kilometres from Alexandria and within striking distance of the vital Suez Canal). During this period it was the perception of Slessor's colleagues and his biographer Geoffrey Dutton, that Slessor's energies and attention as Official War Correspondent had been compromised by the presence of his wife. Dutton's portrayal of Noela is not flattering. She is vacuous, materialistic, adulterous, infantile, dependent, and she couldn't spell. Nevertheless, and despite her affair in Cairo with at least one of Slessor's fellow correspondents, Slessor felt that he could not live without her. They had married young, Noela was only fifteen, Slessor twenty-one, and against their parents' wishes. It was a relationship of mutual dependence, with Slessor as parent and Noela as child 'spoilt and self-absorbed' (to use Dutton's epithets). They had had difficulties before the war, and had separated briefly in the late 1930s. As I mentioned earlier Noela was to die of cancer in 1945, after which Slessor lost the will to write poetry. Dutton paints a picture of Slessor during their time together in the Middle East as a man harried by the provision of suitable lodgings, travel, luxuries, jewellery and emotional support for a woman with a 'whim of iron'. Her constant demands, Dutton believes, preoccupied Slessor so much that his official duties suffered (Dutton, passim). This certainly was borne out by contemporary evidence, including Ian Fitchett, possible one of the people closest to Slessor professionally and personally at this time:

> Ken was very much more occupied with his wife and her safety than with his job. In fact I think his disaster was the presence of his wife Noela in the Middle East. He was devoted to her and she became his number one worry through the time of great panic in Egypt at the time of Rommel's advance when Egypt looked like going. And Ken I'm afraid tended to, well I'm not going to say neglect his job, but without her he would have spent a lot more time with the troops and less with her ... He didn't cover the Battle of Alamein through illness. But without her being there he would certainly not have been in Syria a fortnight before Alamein and would have carried out his job covering the major battle of the Ninth Div which played a major part in the victory of Alamein as Montgomery, Alexander and all of them admitted. (Dutton, 227)

Added to this was the very strong military tradition that it was inimical to soldierly duty to have wives present in a theatre of war. Even Blamey, the Chief in Command of the Australian forces, was criticised for having his wife in Cairo at this time.

The crisis came in October 1942 when Slessor came down with pneumonia after a 'totally unnecessary' (Dutton's words) trip to Lebanon and Palestine, which according to his biographer seemed more like an extended shopping spree rather than a serious attempt to gather material for official despatches. As a result Slessor was in hospital at the start of the battle of El Alamein on 23 October, and was released the day after Rommel ordered a withdrawal of German troops. That he missed this crucial battle was something for which senior officers in the Australian army never forgave him. The consequences were to surface in 1944 after a stinging dispute with Brigadier Windeyer commander of the 20th infantry brigade of the ninth Australian division in Papua New Guinea over Slessor's alleged reporting of the battle for Finschhafen. Slessor has been frustrated by army censorship for some time, but in this case, it was not his own reporting which was in dispute but an inaccurate interview with him which was printed in the *Sydney Sun* in which Slessor appeared to be critical of the conditions under which the men were fighting. Windeyer complained to Divisional Head Quarters in a report which attacked Slessor, in the course of which Windeyer stated that 'during the battle of El Alamein [Slessor] was 'said' to have been in Alexandria ...' (Dutton, 243). That was true, he was suffering from pneumonia, but to anyone with knowledge of Slessor's behaviour at the time this remark carried the clear implication that he was indulging his wife behind the lines while one of the great battles of the Second World War involving Australian troops was being fought. Slessor was livid and from then on crossed swords with Army officialdom, incurring the displeasure of General Blamey, of whom he had a low opinion (witness the poem 'An Inscription for Dog River') which the General had reciprocated ever since Slessor's critical evaluation of Blamey's role in the battle for Crete. The result after some months of tension was that Slessor resigned as Official War Correspondent in February 1944, indicating to his fellow journalist Alexander McDonald some years later that he had 'retired hurt'. The issue which seemed to inflame Slessor the most was the implied allegation of cowardice, or at least neglect of duty, in his *absence* from the El Alamein battlefield.

It is not known when 'Beach Burial' reached its final form. It was published in *Southerly* in 1944. The first signs of its argument and imagery are in the already mentioned account of the La France graves near the Litani River, hundreds of miles from El Alamein. Further processing of the imagery and the dialectic of the poem occur during 1942 and 1943, the last of which is an account of General Auchinleck bathing in the Mediterranean in 1943 which introduces a seaside grave, 'unknown sailors', and clubbing gunfire (Dutton, 251). Significantly, the imagery is that of resurrection, of an emergence of the shining, living body from the dissolving sea of flux which promises something of the last line of the poem, and pointedly he is an ordinary soldier until he puts on the dress of a general:

> A beach in the Gulf of Arabs, two miles from El Alamein, dazzle-white in the morning sunlight and lined with slabs of driftwood over the sandy graves of 'unknown sailors' washed up in dozens with the tide. The guns were clubbing away in the west, and he had come there to swim, and up from the Mediterranean came a naked big-boned man, the water streaming from his hair. He looked like a Scots Guard sergeant major, and until we watched him dress (his aide-de-camp respectfully handing him shorts and shirt) and saw him climb into a waiting jeep, we had not recognised the new commander-in-chief. (Dutton, 231)

We do not know when the poem was finished, but a manuscript exists which shows signs of revision, and that early form of the poem bears the subscript 'El Alamein, 1942' (Dutton, 231) while the printed version leaves out the date. It is this absence of the date which drove me to write this paper. Where Slessor was, on those days on the Battle of El Alamein in 1942, was a very sore point to him. He wasn't at El Alamein as his manuscript version of the date invites us to infer. He was back in Alexandria, and he was not witness to the events which produced so many deaths. Equally disturbing about this poem, placed and dated to refer to an epic land battle, is the fact that it deals with the results of a sea battle somewhere other than the Gulf of Arabs (which Slessor's despatch places at two miles from El Alamein) – the convoys of dead have made their way to a landfall here. They too have turned up long after a battle, mute testimony to its waste and horror. The sense of alienation and distance from the actual events, which produced this outcome, and the process and purpose behind it, is palpable. The ghostly pencil wavers (changed from 'quivers' in manuscript) and fades. There is no way this observer can share in or make sense of who or what they are: they are 'unknown seamen'.

It must have struck Slessor when he was preparing this poem for publication after his acrimonious resignation as Official War Correspondent that 'El Alamein 1942' was too precise a set of co-ordinates for this poem. After all he was not there then. But he had been at El Alamein after the battle and wrote movingly in his despatches about its aftermath: the wreckage, the graves, the corpses, the confusion (Dutton, 168–9; Slessor, v). In the 1960s Slessor wrote about the poem (mainly for school-children), and in these notes one can sense the care with which he covers the material I have just rehearsed and the reticence and pain associated with this episode:

> 'Beach Burial' comes from the period when Australian soldiers were fighting in the Western Desert of Egypt near El Alamein, where the German advance had been halted in 1942. Many of their camps were on the Mediterranean coast, and in the morning it was not uncommon to find the bodies of drowned men washed up on the beaches. They were buried in the sandhills under improvised crosses, identification usually being impossible. Most of them were sailors, some British, some German or Italian, some of them 'neutrals'. (Semmler, 447–8)

He ends by explaining how 'enlisted on the other front' may be read:

> Many of the inquiries from students about this poem have asked the meaning of its last words *'other front'*. The superficial meaning, of course, is a military one. The verses were written at a time when there was pressure on the Allies to open a 'second front' against the Germans.
>
> However, there is a deeper implication which is really the theme of the poem. It is the idea that all men of all races, whether they fight with each other or not, are engaged together on the common 'front' of humanity's existence. The absolute fact of death unites them. Their hatreds, quarrels and wars should be dwarfed by the huger human struggle to survive against disease and cataclysms on this dangerous planet. (Slessor, 139)

In reaching for the universals this reading depends on, Slessor was unconsciously reinforcing what he had done in the creative act of the poem itself, creating another, metaphysical front, to replace the physical one he had so unfortunately missed. As Dutton says 'one can only guess at Slessor's conscience over all this. An inner turmoil may have contributed to several problems with his health at this time, culminating in his bout of pneumonia.' (Slessor, 139)

Bad conscience perhaps produced this other front of reconciliation and hope which had so spectacularly been enacted before him by the emergence of Auchinleck from the sea. But I would like to conclude this paper by suggesting a reason other than bad conscience: the role of war correspondent itself.

When Slessor was appointed Official War Correspondent out of a field of fifty other journalists, Ian Fitchett, who was acting in the position at the time, summarised Slessor's view of the job as 'a poet's view of the Anzac tradition' (Dutton, 228), and Frank Ashton of Associated Newspapers wrote as well that it was a fitting appointment as he had always regarded Slessor 'as one of the most outstanding descriptive writers in Australia'

(Dutton, 179). These are significant observations. Slessor's journalism in *Smith's Weekly* and *The Sun* was indeed descriptive, and often what could be called in photographic terms 'picturesque'. His equivalent in that mode of representation would be Frank Hurley, who photographed Australian troops in both world wars. Hurley's style was that of 'Nature methodised'. The message was more important than reality – grubby and difficult to control as it was. His photo montages and elaborate stagings of events certainly captured some of the grandeur of the Antarctic and the desert campaigns of World War One, but he was a different generation from most of the photographers of World War Two, notably Damien Parer who won an Oscar for his coverage of the Kokoda campaign, grubby and difficult as that was, by shooting his material in the front-line. Slessor was no Chester Wilmot or Gavin Long. Even without the distraction of Noela he was a reflective writer whose polished and decorated prose bore all the marks of his studied Parnassian poetry of the 1920s and the early 1930s.

While Slessor's despatches show that he really believed in the Anzac myth and the dignity and heroism of the common Australian soldier (despite witnessing some despicable acts by them in Greece), Slessor was not a 'realist' in the mode of many intellectuals and artists of the 1930s. His sensibility was that of the late nineteenth century and his art reflected the tensions which that produced when confronted with the anxieties of the revolution in thought and art of the early twentieth century. As Official War Correspondent he wasn't Damien Parer with a hand-held Bell and Howell Eyemo on the invasion beach at Peleliu dying from a machine gun bullet, but the reflective poet too late for the battle watching the dead bodies from a long-decided encounter roll around in the surf from which had materialised the shining, resurrected body of a General. The other front was indeed one where war could be memorialised in a tableau of the picturesque, where brother embraced brother in a montage worthy of Hurley, and he could enlist their experience to speak to others of their suffering and sacrifice.

Although he had missed the battle, and had struggled hard to communicate the experience of war, he was well aware of his failure to join with the combatants because of personal crises (bodily and emotional), and through his profession as an official observer and fabricator of works of art. It was with those works of art, the metaphysical other front of universals where all could be resolved in a satisfying unity, which he had to content himself.

Texts cited

Croft, Julian. "The Nothing That is Neither Long Nor Short: Slessor and Silence", in Philip Mead (ed.), *Kenneth Slessor: Critical Readings*, St Lucia, University of Queensland Press, 1997.

Dutton, Geoffrey. *Kenneth Slessor: A Biography*, Ringwood, Victoria, Viking, 1991.

Semmler, Clement (ed.). *The War Despatches of Kenneth Slessor: Official Australian Correspondent 1940–1944*, St Lucia, University of Queensland Press, 1987.

Slessor, Kenneth. *Poems*, Sydney, Angus and Robert-son, 1963.

The Burial

SATENDRA NANDAN
UNIVERSITY OF CANBERRA

My brother announced, 'We must attend the funeral. At all costs,' he added.

The time, day and date were announced on the radio several times, after every local news bulletin. On the morning of the funeral it was mentioned that the final rites will be performed at the Vatuwaqa cemetery, Suva Point, by Pundit Baikunth Nath Sharma.

'We've to leave early – before sunrise,' ordered Bhaiwa. 'The cremation is at 1 pm sharp. The harvesting gang will have a holiday tomorrow.'

My brother was the sirdar of the sugar-cane cutting gang. He had studied up to class eight in the local school; he was arguably the most educated farmer in the village. And no-one argued with him, as he strode the fields with a sharpened cane-knife.

That evening, as the cane-cutters were returning from day's work on the fields of sugarcane that stretched from the seashores to the jagged mountain range, I was dispatched to call my cousin Rama aka Diesel. Rama drove our International cargo lorry which carted tonnes of sugarcane to Lautoka Mill. He was faster than the locomotive which hauled loaded trucks of freshly harvested cane over the pakki lines set next to the corrugated, dusty road, built by our girmit grandparents, with potholes as deep as children's graves.

Rama took great pride in driving the International, the biggest lorry in the village. A red-flag fluttered from the bonnet of the lorry as the driver sat at an angle on the driver's seat with a rubber cushion below his ample buttocks. In the dashboard he kept a small red plastic idol of Hanuman.

Personally I was proud of Rama's driving.

Bhaiwa told him to check diesel, oil, water and tyres. 'And don't forget the tool-box, launda!' he warned.

Next morning as the sun shone across the mist-laden peaks and green fields, anastomosis between swaying palm fronds, with cooking smoke rising from the kitchens of the farmers and cane-cutters, four of us – Rama, Bhaiwa, Solomoni, and I – left via the airport road for Suva. I felt warm on a cold oneiric June morning squeezed between Solomoni and Bhaiwa who was holding the hand-brake, rather tightly and quite unnecessarily.

As the sun rose higher, Rama put on his dark sunglasses, the cargo lorry jumped over pot-holes and strewn sugarcane on the road. Near Yako koro, he almost ran over a black sow with a line of five pink piglets following their mother.

'Magainichi!' a voice yelled from one of the dark bures of the koro. Rama pressed the accelerator.

He glanced at Solomoni who smiled and then asked Bhaiwa to tell us the story of the man whose funeral we were on our way to attend in Suva, in a cargo lorry. Bhaiwa looked pensive; his grey hair shone in the rays of the sun, his thick, trimmed moustache was illuminated intermittently as we passed over hills covered with pine trees and under raintrees thatching part of the Queen's Road.

'No-one,' my brother said, 'had more degrees than Chinnappa's son. Or more medals or honours given to him. He was the first indentured labourer's son who was made a knight by Queen Victoria.'

'Queen Elizabeth,' corrected Solomoni.

'Queen Elizabeth the Second,' I insisted.

I was studying history in Form V and my history teacher was Ratu Reddy, Baijubawara's only son. And Ratu's history lessons were like inscriptions on tombstones, dead and indelible. 'The mind,' he'd said, 'was a tabula rasa, like tablas' he added for originality.

Chinnappa's son, Chinna was lying in the cold mortuary at CWM Hospital. My brother was determined to tell us the story of this most remarkable man from our little, obscure village named Lega Lega adjacent to the smallest airport on the fatal shores of the largest ocean.

∞

Cousin Rama Narayan switched off the radio in his lorry and Bhiawa began the tale as we passed the bridge, damaged by recent floods; the road was covered with debris. The mayor, it seemed, had migrated to New Zealand with the cleaning money. Everyone admired how he'd cleaned the coffers of the township.

'He was my classmate at Mulomulo. We studied together. His father had come from Rakiraki and I'd had given him a piece of my land to build a bure,' began Bhaiwa.

'Chinnappa was a fine cane-cutter. He lived in that one bure with his wife, two children, a son name Chinpaiyya Murgalingam Gounder and a daughter Princess Sarojini Naidu.'

This was unusual as most girmit people had only a single name. But I didn't interrupt Bhaiwya. He didn't like interruptions, especially from school boys.

'How now?' enquired Solomoni. 'All these three-four barrelled names with Maharaj, Sharma, Gosai, Aryan, Chaudhary, Padayachi .... '

Before Solomoni could finish the lineage, Bhaiwa shouted, 'Chamartaliya Chutias, yaar!'

'Anyway,' continued my brother, looking at the bananas, pawpaws, crabs and fish being sold by the road side, 'Chinpaiyya and I grazed Lali together. We ploughed and hoed the land; we planted cane; we watered the vegetable seedlings near the well. And we sat together under tamarind trees and ate a lot of sugarcane. His teeth were strong and white – whiter than white sugar.'

Here Bhaiwa bared his set of white teeth. Solomoni closed his mouth firmly and gulped.

The yellow sun, like a slice of pineapple, was above the pine trees.

'Sometimes we sang bhajans,' said Bhaiwa. 'He was good at playing dandtaal.'

'And then,' said Bhiawa, 'the floods came: it rained in sheets. The wild winds from the mountain blew across our village. The river was in full spate: it was a sight to see. Its strong current in the middle and the rush of water, so powerful, so potent. To see a river in its full potency is to understand the holiness of Ganga. Brown water swirling over the raintrees tearing the banks of the Nandi.'

To us the river was our life-line. After the rain we went to the banks, near Kalpu nana's kund next to Molowai koro, with empty sugar sacks and collected fruits and vegetables: pawpaws, coconuts, breadfruit, bananas, oranges, watermelons floating down towards the insatiable sea.

Occasionally we saw a carcass in the midstream with a mynah bird sitting on it, blissfully unaware of death, its yellow beak shining in the sun.

'The floods fascinated and frightened us,' continued Bhaiwa.

'Then during one season of the floods, something extraordinary happened. It had rained incessantly for three days. We couldn't cross the river to go and see how people had survived on the other bank.'

'Do you remember it, Solomoni?' asked my brother in the gentlest tone.

'O Mahendoni, I can never forget that flood!'

For when the flood subsided, Solomoni was found clinging to the topmost branch of a half-fallen raintree that had spread its branches far and wide. We used to play on its huge trunk and fish from its leaning branches touching the waters of the Nandi. It shaded the water, it sheltered us. And the little fishes cooled under it.

During the flood his village had been washed away. Solomoni had climbed on top of the tallest bure for two nights and remained there.

Early the third morning the thatched part of the bure unaligned itself and floated in the flooded river.

Solomoni sat on top until the drenched roof hit the branch of a mighty big raintree, bent by the flood, broken by a landslide. Solomoni held a branch of the raintree and climbed to the topmost branch.

He saw the waters swirl menacingly. And when my brother rescued him, he was clinging to the branch as if he were part of the tree.

Solomoni and Bhaiwa became closest of companions. A bure was erected by the villagers for Solomoni, next to our own three bures on the CSR Company's sugarcane farm. It was inherited by my father after the death of his father, our girmit grandfather.

Girmit, we were told by Ratu Reddy, was gulami, slavery with an expiry date, although Ratu couldn't remember any dates.

The farm was the freest place on which we grew, and the years by the river flowed. We were like logs floating towards the same ocean, buffeted from one bank to another.

Solomoni was taken to Nadi hospital on our horse Charlie. He clung to my brother's shoulder as they rode double-bank to the Nadi Health Centre with Vuniwai Sadhu in sole charge with a big brown nurse in a white cap and purple dress and black sandals.

Sadhu poured a pinkish mixture from a large bottle into a smaller one and handed it to Solomoni.

'Drink this three times a day,' he instructed Solomoni who showed his gratitude by standing up, holding the bottle with his two large hands.

Bhaiwa began pestering Sadhu with questions: Should he drink this before meal? Can he continue to have his grog? Can he eat something with the mixture?

Sadhu growled, 'He can eat anything! And, you chutia launda, just don't eat my head!'

Solomoni and Bhaiwa left the Vuniwai's office in a great haste and forgot to ride Charlie home. My cousin Rama was sent to fetch the horse in the late evening when Sadhu was ensconced inside his green government quarters eating gifts given to him as ghoose.

Solomoni remained in one of the bures for a whole week, drinking skimmed milk, eating mountains of thickly grained, steam-boiled rice, dhal and bhaji.

When he recovered, we discovered he was from a small koro up in the hills beyond Nasua and Sablau.

Bhaiwa said, as we approached Deuba, that it was a miracle two people were saved in the Big Toofan.

'Who was the other one, Bhaiwa?' asked Solomoni with interest.

'It was Chinnappa, Solomoni,' revealed Bhaiwa in a quiet tone with a wink.

∞

Apparently Chinnappa, after the cane-cutting season, had opened a grog shop on the edges of Nandi Airport. The local coolumber, Mr Sim Sim, came to his house often for a bowl of freshly squeezed yagona from his tinned bangla. Chinnappa quickly picked up a few words of English, and with a mixture of Hindi, Fijian, English, he could compose a colourful sentence. He began conversing with the coolumber: 'Bula, Sahibji. Long time not seeing? How you going?'

Sim Sim began to appreciate Chinnappa's entrepreneurial spirit and enthusiasm for the language of the Greatest Empire.

Mr Sim Sim was a big man, physically. And he ran some gravel business with a man named Nandu Maharaj. Sim Sim and he were supplying gravel from Nadi river, close to our village, to the airport tarmac under construction. Every morning huge lorries roared up the hill with wet gravel freshly dredged from the Nandi's placid waters. Our little road, littered with potholes, would become wet and muddy. And we ran behind the lorries.

There was a single crane digging and loading the lorries with gravel. Sim Sim enjoyed Chinnappa's grog so much that he offered him the job of a watchman – to look after the crane – 'zhaam', from 6 pm to 6 am every night of the week.

Chinnappa said to us, 'Chandriya night or churaiya night, Chinnappa is always there, sitting by the zhaam with his plastic basin grog full.'

The night of the big flood, when Nadi town's wooden bridge was washed away and most of the shops were under water, that night Chinnappa forgot all about the crane! Next morning when there was a let up in the rain, he went to check on the crane. He was shocked to see swirling waters in murderous colours on the spot where the crane was supposed to be, solid and immovable.

Chinnappa said he became 'cane-crazy' – running up and down the wet, muddy banks like a dog who had seen his master go under the water. Then, as he slipped and fell towards the flooded river, he saw the top part of the crane visible in swirling waters. Two mynah birds were cheeping on top of it.

Chinnappa jumped from the bank and swam to the crane: he clung to the top, his hair muddy, his clothes wet. As an afterthought, he tore the front of his white shirt. He looked like a man who had tried to save something precious without caring for his life. Slowly, he tightened his grip on the crane and shouted for Bhaiwa.

Bhaiwa and Solomoni rushed down the slope and came and stood on the river's bank. Chinnappa looked like a man in despair, close to drowning.

And Mr Sim Sim came in his jeep with large, muddy, black gum boots.

'Bula!' shouted Solomoni.

'Salaam Sahibji,' greeted Bhaiwa.

But Sim Sim's cunning, coolumber gaze was focused on Chinnappa, hanging on the crane like a black bat from a mango tree.

'Hey, Chinna,' he called into the flooded river. 'You there throughout the rains. You didn't let go the crane? Oh, Chinna! Phew!'

He looked at Bhaiwa and Solomoni with tears in his eyes.

Chinnappa suddenly shouted, 'Is in my dootie, Sir!'

'Never say die!' interjected Solomoni.

'Duty is Duty Chinna,' shouted back Sim Sim. 'Oh Chinna! What a man!'

He again looked at Solomoni and Bhaiwa, as if they were children of some lesser gods; certainly in his eyes they were lesser men.

'Come down, now man,' pleaded Sim Sim, 'taking you to hospital! Oh my God!.'

Sim Sim's admiration knew no bounds. Then Chinna shouted; 'Me no swimming, Sahib!'

Mr Sim Sim hired a motor boat and sent Lesu and Blooma to get Chinnappa off the crane.

When Chinnappa finally came to the river's bank, Mr Sim Sim clasped his hand and helped him off the boat. We all marveled at his devotion to duty. He was driven to the hospital, sitting next to Mr Sim Sim in his jeep.

'He'll get a medal,' commented Solomoni. 'Just wait for Queen's Birthday Honours, Bhaiwa.'

'Only much later,' continued Bhaiwa, 'we learnt the true story as narrated by Chinnappaiya himself.'

It seems during the heavy rains Chinna had slept and forgotten all about the crane. Only after two nights, he remembered to go and look for the 'bloody zhaam'. But the crane had disappeared; he was desperate. As he ran up and down the river's bank, he saw a steel piece sticking out of the flooded river in Kalpu's kund.

He dived into the muddy waters, swam to the top of the crane, tore his shirt, muddied his hair, and then shouted for Bhaiwa.

'Boyo,' he said to me, 'big bullshit raining, mountain flooding!' Me sleeping with your fat mausi. Close to her stomach. Forgetting all about the white man's bloody zhaam!'

Soon after Chinnappa's only son was given a CSR scholarship to Tasmania. Years later, He returned as a barrister and solicitor. It all sounded very impressive, although none of us knew the difference and Ratu Reddy didn't explain. He simply said that the world has produced only one lawyer: MK Gandhi, Attorney-General.

∞

Chinnappa became our village pujari. He created a strange structure of bamboo poles under the mango tree. In it he wove multi-coloured ribbons and cotton threads. A few murtis – idols made of clay – were placed in the sacred place. Soon he was in great demand and traveled to Tavua, Rakiraki and Sigatoka performing Goinda ceremonies.

As adolescents Rama and I were fascinated by the pujari's antics. Near our home was a hillock with a large, craggy rock. Every Sunday, while well-dressed Christians from the Molowai koro went to their church, near the airport, Chinnappa, clad in his saffron loongi, a kind of wrap-around seeped in turmeric, marched towards the hill beating his drum of goat's skin. With a mala round his neck, ash marks on his forehead, and a red scarf covering his hair, he looked quite striking to our young eyes. He called his hill the Holi Hill.

Rama and I followed him at a safe distance, occasionally hiding in the rows of sugarcane. Chinnappa, on reaching the top of the hill, would dig a large hole with a 'sippee', chop a few mango kindlings, put marigold and hibiscus petals round the dug hole. Then he'd leepo-poto it with Lali's fresh dung which he had carried in an aluminum pot, given to him by Trikambhai, the local shopkeeper, owner of a liquor shop. He'd then blow his conch-shell seven times.

Chinnappa would mumble mantras in Hindi, Tamil, Fijian and Sanskrit giving the ancient language a special island rhythm. We didn't understand a word of it but Rama always bowed his head when the mantras were chanted. After every few mixed mantras, Chinnappa would shout 'Oma Soaha' loudly over the gentle shivering cane tops. Mangal's dogs would howl in response. His puja would end with Bula Vinaka, Ni Sa Moce, Om Shanti hurled over our heads.

We'd emerge from the sugarcane field and greet him with folded palms. Once you showed him respect and recognised his prowess as a pujari, Chinnappa treated you with great kindness. He would give us prasad – sultanas mixed with white sugar! Our only interest in the ceremony was the prasad.

This became our Sunday ritual and, when on some Sundays, Chinnappa didn't perform the puja, we felt quite bereft.

∞

One Sunday Chinnappa told us to invite all the children of the village.

'They must be there at 10 o'clock,' he said with a Sanskrit twang. 'I'm performing a special puja. Plenty of prasad for all. Be on top of Holi Hill.'

Rama and I went to rural houses – small bures and tin sheds – and whispered instructions to our classmates and cowherd companions.

We arrived before him. A fire pit was smouldering. Soon we saw him coming up the hill, a holy figure. As he came to the top, all of us were stunned into complete silence. Rama asked us to sit quietly as one by one the village boys and girls arrived around the burning pit. The sun was bright in the sky and the hole of ceremony was glowing with embers of mango kindlings. On one side of the hole were planted two banana leaves, slightly wilted but the singed beauty of the leaves made us feel more holy. Near them were place prasad: sugar and sultanas, halwa, gulgulas and a few other sweet-meats from Trikambhai's wife.

As the smoke rose from the pit, Chinnappa stood up, his red loongi like the tail of Hanuman, touching the earth. His body had red, yellow and saffron marks and his face was heavily powdered. On his forehead was the large, round mark with turmeric and a few grains of brown rice.

Chinnappa didn't smile at any of us. He looked serious and we sensed something important will be performed. Next to the prasad lay a garland of marigold, hibiscus and frangipani petals. He had, I noticed, developed a 'churki' – the old version of a modern pony-tail of sorts. From the 'churki' two brilliantly coloured petals of bougainvilleas hung like paper flowers.

Chinnappa sat by the fire-pit. The hole was much bigger than we'd seen before. He recited a mixture of mantras from ancient texts, (it seemed he memorised these from B.N. Sharma's 'pothas' sold in Fiji bookshops). Baikunth Nath Sharma had written a number of these for priests and pundits giving the ceremonies some order, sequence and intelligibility. For this service he'd received an award from Mauritius.

After hurling several shoklas in every direction, he poured a bowl of kava from a beer bottle. Then he sat silent for fifteen minutes: only his lips moved, his eyes were closed in a yogic pose. The sun shone like a torch on his bare skin, smooth and oily.

After his meditation, he called us to come nearer the smouldering pit. On our forehead he put red marks and then said something miraculous:

'Today, I've decided to walk on fire!'

With these stunning words he turned his face from us and took out a saffron bag, and out of it a large serve of halwa and spread if over the burning fire. The ghee in the halwa made the fire crackle and the flames shot up toward the yellow sun: the flames of freedom.

The children were absolutely silent. We dreaded the fire-walking ceremony: how can a man walk on fire? On red embers glowing in the burning sun.

Then Chinnappa did something extraordinary. He lay his bare back – from the nape of his neck to the small of his back – on the glowing ash-covered embers, his head and legs outside the hole of fire. He must have lain for a few seconds, when the silence was shattered by a piercing scream.

Suddenly he jumped up, his loongi fell and he ran utterly naked and dived into the pond where we used to bathe Lali. We ran into the sugar-cane fields.

After about an hour Chinnappa, our pujari, was walking up the small hill, his caste marks washed away, the garland gone; he wearing a pair of khaki shorts.

He came and sat near Rama. He said things had gone wrong. The holy fire had been polluted. The halwa, as he lay, had stuck to his left buttock and had burnt a black hole. He couldn't bear the pain of his skin being scalded by hot halwa and embers.

We listened in sheer amazement. He said he'd to go to Labasa to learn the mantras for fire-walking ceremony during Ram Lila.

He told us, his banar sena, we'd get special sweets today, as long as no rumours were spread in the village.

We sat and ate a lot of halwa and prasad. The fire was extinguished by Rama. And as Chinnappa marched in front, Rama behind him touching the red welt on his bare back, we, the village kids, walked behind these two miracle men.

One by one, the village children disappeared unseen, unnoticed by their parents. I, too, suddenly felt lonely, knowing that Chinnappa would not be performing this ceremony for a long time. But he'd attempted to give us some idea of a miracle – walking on fire – in our drab and dreary daily life.

Rama became his friend and Bhaiwa employed Chinnappa as a cane-cutter on the farm. But this man had a fiery vision. He opened the first grog shop near the airport and created the first local lawyer in his son.

∞

Early next morning I rushed to the river. A river has many streams, many sources, my girmit grandfather had told us. Now that he was dead, his ashes in the ocean, I began to see the streams as human stories.

And as I walked to the school the sun shone on billiard green sugarcane fields, the cane-knives glinting in the morning sun. Most of the cane-cutters had large sweat-stained felt hats on their heads. Their faces were marked like holes in an abandoned hornets' nest. And their feet were bare, their hands looked strong and large.

I arrived a minute before Ratu Reddy entered the classroom. He was wearing a white shirt, starched and ironed, black trousers with a colourful belt, brown shoes with red socks, which matched with a black and red tie knotted tightly. Ratu was a darkish man with a balding round head. Perspirations would appear on his lips as he taught and occasionally his emotions overran historical facts. He was a story teller with a dyed black moustache.

This morning he came to the class with the daily Times in his right hand. He looked unusually sober and subdued. He didn't say, 'Gooda Morning class' and sat on the chair.

Instead he stood against the edge of the brown-timbered table made by Popular Paradise Furnitures.

'Class,' he began, 'today I'll tell you about great men in the world.' And, he paused: 'One such person was a student of this very school.'

We were wondering who that could be, when Vidya Sagar, sitting behind me, yelled, 'Hilary-Tenzing!'

Ratu said, 'They were foreigners.'

'But this morning I'll read to you an obituary of a famous man of Fiji – a self-made man, shaped by this school. The story of Chinnappaiya Gounder must be an inspiration to you all.'

He looked at me sharply, adjusting his round spectacles on his bulbous nose. I recalled he'd told us that God gave us a nose so that we could wear glasses for reading not sunglasses for showing off. Some of my friends wore sunglasses at night.

He began: Chinnappaiya Gounder was born in a humble hut; his father was a cane-cutter; later he progressed to a watchman and opened a grog shop near Nandi International airport. He did it all for his son's education. Yesterday, his son Chinnappaiya Gounder alias Sir Charles Gordon, was buried in Suva cemetery – one of the largest funerals in the national capital. The Chief Justice and the Attorney-General gave speeches. And many lawyers had come in black and white looking like penguins with wigs.

The word 'buried' jolted me into a new consciousness. Bhaiwa, Solomoni, Rama and I had attended his cremation at Vatuwaqa Cemetery.

Ratu read two paragraphs from the obituary about his education in Tasmania and his contribution to the debates in Legco.

'And,' continued our history teacher, 'why did he change his names to Charles Gordon?'

No hands went up in the class.

'Well, let me tell you. He was inspired by the life and work of Charles Freer Andrews, a discipline of Gandhiji and Sir Arthur Gordon, the first Governor of our Crown colony.'

We'd never heard of CF Andrews, nor of Sir Arthur Gordon. Gandhiji's name was vaguely familiar through a film song. Ratu Reddy sensed something was amiss – perhaps he had spent too much time teaching us the history of the greatest Empire, and too little time on the history of our own country.

'Fiji,' he said, 'was ceded, not conquered. The Deed of Cession made all the difference,' he added.

'Indian indentured labourers were brought in from obscure villages in India to work on the plantations owned by the CSR company of Australia. They came in 87 ships – that number is important, auspicious,' he emphasised.

Ratu couldn't recall the exact number of people who were transported. He rattled the details of caste, religions, regions. I was falling half asleep – history to me was what the white historians wrote in books from which we'd to pass the Senior Cambridge examination.

Ratu was telling us, 'Sir Charles Gordon was a mirror of our lives. His pyre lit our lives, illuminated a generation ....'

I was in a reverie: Did 'burial' and 'cremation' mean the same thing: Death?

The dead keep forgiving us endlessly in our ignorance.

∞

And Solomoni had solemnly uttered at the end of the creation, 'Bula Vinaka, Mahendoni!'

And my brother had said, 'Moths are born in darkness. They die in the flames of a dhebri because they see only darkness in the heart of light.'

I didn't have the heart to tell my village brother that we really hadn't attended the cremation of Chinnapaiyya Gounder, aka Sir Charles Gordon, son of Chinnappa.

We had, in fact, gone to the wrong funeral.

Sir Charles was, in truth, buried.

When

VINCENT O'SULLIVAN
VICTORIA UNIVERSITY

When a woman with flaming hair
enough to read by, write by,
left me for 'Fame', neither of us
taking in how memory's tacky enough
amber would hold us for a long time yet,
an Aussie friend, with the kindest
intentions, said 'Come to lunch at Olga's,'
Olga's being an Adelaide restaurant
whose staff wore 'night attire',
see-though gauze or whatever, eye-level
distraction for the broken-hearted
while one ordered 'Shrimps, thank you,'
or 'Today's catch: barramundi.'

There was no irony much when you eat
at Olga's. What you saw was what
you didn't get, but one bloke to another,
a thoughtful deed had been done.
The irony came later, taking its time
to marinade. I'm reading a book
that says how Percy Grainger would have
liked 'to write music like the Adelaide
hills.' The friend who took me
to lunch (this is a long time after)
has trouble with his eyes. The woman who
provoked my mate's good turn won't leave
where she is now, wherever that is.
I never heard the final line. The pub
though where Grainger lived is still
there, I like knowing that. And the music.
The hills. The fires, sooner or later.

Performances in Review: Reviews in Performance

MURRAY BRAMWELL
FLINDERS UNIVERSITY

Repressed Memory: Back to My Roots and Other Suckers

Barry Humphries, Her Majesty's.
The Adelaide Review, No. 238, July, 2003, p. 20.

Barry Humphries is not only back to his roots but also quite a few of his old tricks. Playing to full houses for a short season at Her Majesty's, Humphries has rounded up the usual suspects for our delectation and occasional panic. These now include somebody called Barry Humphries. Not *the* Barry Humphries I shouldn't think, but a simulacrum who, last time around, appeared from a camphor box full of Proustian prompts, and this time introduces a Dunnathon – old Super8 (and almost suppurating) home movies of Glen Iris in 1949. Alf Dunn, Humphries would have us believe, was a neighbour of his family and his films chronicle, in long Warhol-esque wide-shot, primary school sports days, social gatherings, even the end of year party. That's me as a rather young Father Christmas, Humphries informs us, and we are inclined to believe him.

Back to the roots for Humphries, and much of his audience, means back to suburban memory – of brand names, street names and the sounds and mnemonic smells of Times Past. These times, when they constituted the Present for Barry Humphries as a young and impatient bohemian, signified a stultifying world of trivia and small-minded gentility. It was the world of his parents and part of the dreary trade-off for post-war prosperity. Here was the original version of Relaxed and

Comfortable – Edna, Sandy and the *Herald* waiting on the front lawn.

But there are also others who drag the past resolutely into the future. Take Sir Les Patterson for instance: although most of us would rather not. This drunken, priapic praiser of his own past is the cultural attaché for Misrule and a friend to the Arts, if he is to be taken on his own account. Les is Humphries' most dangerous creation. His cheerful bigotry is more a part of Humphries' satiric strategy than convivial comedy but quite a few in the audience nevertheless take his cue to chortle heartlessly at easy targets. It is disconcerting to hear such unreconstructed hilarity but, as Les would be the first to tell you, comedy alas is not a precision tool.

Barry Humphries regularly likes to have a swipe or two at the corporate types, as he describes them. Last time it was an IOC hanger-on. This time Owen Steele is a bland, self-serving CEO tiptoeing through a general meeting of peeved shareholders. It is a point well-made but Humphries has no particular intensity for his subject and there is less of the usual heat-seeking ruthlessness in it all.

The Sandy Stone soliloquy at the end of the first half is, by contrast, his most theatrical. Sandy is swept out in a spray of white light and fog – his throne a Genoa velvet armchair piled on a stack of hard rubbish waiting on the ghostly median strip at Gallipoli Crescent for the looters in utes to come by. Sandy is long dead now but his wraith meditates in a slightly bewildered way about the passing of what once was. His widow Beryl has done her dough on HIH shares and life in Surfers is not looking so good for her after all. Also, the site of Sandy's house, having already made way for a supermarket, is now being cleared again for a series of Tuscan style town houses. Sandy ruminates on the increasing rarity of the fourteen essential oils in Rexona soap and the availability of the Incontinence Helpline. Sandy is Humphries' most dreamy character whose dithery otherworldliness seems to capture more – of both his creator and the ageing audience – each time he is wheeled out for a nice night's entertainment.

The appearance of Dame Edna, however, is the real centre of Humphries' show. Flanked by the Ednaettes, she offers sizzling burlesque. The front rows cower and Edna surveys her quarry like a hawk looking for fieldmice. I don't pick on people, she whinnies triumphantly, I empower them. This time she empowers a sampling of women – one a public servant, whose occupation raises compulsive laughter for an audience increasingly hysterical and likely to sacrifice members of their own family to escape or desperately mollify the rampaging Edna. A young couple are dragged on stage while Edna endeavours to salvage what she presumes to be their wrecked marriage. The bride's father is also brought on for additional humiliation.

Edna then assembles the luckless draftees to perform excerpts of volume two of her autobiography, and like the good sports people are in impossible situations, they neither attempt to be funnier than permitted nor run screaming to an exit which is probably the sane thing to do. Having despatched her cast, Edna muses yet again upon her celebrity and her underachieving family. It is familiar territory but Humphries has, as ever, a keen eye for the latest bogusness and an ear for the most recently excruciating jargon.

Then, as tradition requires, Dame Edna sings a song, dances a jig and slings as many gladiolus plumes as she can to the furthest corners of the theatre. This is her benediction and her final fling as theatrical dominatrix. You adore me – and I quite like you, she crows superciliously and, one suspects, a little more of Mr Humphries appears from behind the mask. He is, however, an extraordinary presence.

There are few performers anywhere who can single-handedly animate a stage the way Barry Humphries can. And Edna, in particular, is a force of nature. She may not have come back to her roots – neither she nor Barry Humphries have the slightest interest in, or notion of, contemporary Australia – but she knows the art of the pinch and the punch and the Chinese burn. Which must mean we are her other suckers – queuing up in the best tradition of comedy to be railed against and humiliated, and then to be handed a gladiolus, this mad version of a vertical garland, as consolation for our tears.

Fifty Years Young: Back with a Vengeance

Barry Humphries, Her Majesty's. *The Adelaide Review*, No. 320, July 6, 2007, p. 19.

Barry Humphries is celebrating fifty years as a music hall artiste. In 1957 Mrs Everage from Moonie Ponds first peered around the door with her beady eyes and imperious curiosity to say hello. She really was a housewife then, with dull straight hair and a drab cloth coat, but she knew aqua from duck-egg blue and of course, her prudery and pretensions have only magnified over the decades. Barry Humphries' now monstrous megastar strides the globe in a blizzard of self-serving celebrity and she is back, at Her Majesty's, with a vengeance.

For Edna it is the same vengeance as always – to be the biggest star, to have the glitziest outfit ('Jane Lomax Smith will copy this frock,' she shrieks in a twirl of titanium lamé) and to have the coolest entourage. The Edna-Tones, doubling as personal trainers, pilates instructors and personal security, display their well-toned pecs and rumps while Dame Edna makes a complete spectacle of herself.

The opening number, staged in her New York penthouse, gives way to archive footage of the Dame while Barry Humphries' other incarnation Les Patterson prepares to take the stage. If Edna comes from Forties variety, Les is straight out of Aristophanes. With his jackass teeth spraying saliva on the front rows and his donkey-schlong prominent in his trouser line, he is the antic fool of all vulgarity, bluer than any duck, and, tonight, ready to bone his way to the top of Channel Nine. Les is replete from a feed at Hog's Breath and a round with his personal assistant. 'I'm fuller than a Macquarie Banker's wallet, he announces, I'm sweating like a glass blower's arse.'

Les has been having visitations – from the ghost of Kerry Packer. He's worried the changes at Nine aren't working – 'Eddie McGuire wouldn't know a tram was up him till the bell rang.' Sir Les, man of the world and connoisseur of the consular trough is now also needed in the board room. He is brilliantly revolting, startlingly crass – as once Humphries satirised Australian primness, now he makes fun of our sophistication. Les is as embarrassing as phone-camera footage of a union rep, as unwelcome as a trouser cough at a Hillsong service.

Sandy Stone returns to close the first half: welcome adagio to the frenetic movements of Dame Edna and Les, the ghost of Glen Iris slumps into the genoa velvet club lounge. A shade beneath the shade, he brings us up to speed on the progress of his widow, Beryl. She has fallen on hard times since the death of her second beau Clarrie Lockwood. The tidy sum he left her for her days at Tudor Mews have been swindled by Rhonda from Mumbai and Beryl is now in a federally-funded facility, surrounded by indifferent young 'operatives' plugged in to iPods, sinking further into the twilight zone.

It is the grimmest view yet on Sandy's world and even the nostalgia for brand names and the relaxed and comfortable fifties has been truncated. As Sandy talks about the Japs and Abos, Humphries dangles the bait towards audience which, when it bites, reminds us that humour is amoral and the true comedian is no-one's friend.

Act Two is all Edna, and Humphries' energy and invention remains a marvel. Edna rattles through her current exploits, skiting and name-dropping. 'I am comfortable in my own skin', she whinnies, as she tells us that the Queen has a lovely sense of humour which doesn't show on the coins.

The inevitable occurs as Edna prowls the audience. I'm not picking on you, I am empowering you, she crows, while interrogating Patricia about her house at Victor and Cecily about her unit in Glenelg. Humphries wickedly exploits the post-code snobbery as Edna derides the responses even as the show depends on the participation. An interesting reversal occurs with the compatible DNA matching of David and Lorraine whose marriage is being arranged onstage. When Edna asks why he is amused, David matter-of-factly informs her that he is gay – to the deafening cheer of the audience. It is a brilliant turning point in the dynamics of the comedy and a reminder that honesty can never be ridiculed.

After the hilarious gospel spoof – 'What will be My Legacy?' – Edna begins firing gladioli into the crowd, up to the paupers in the circle and into the front rows. As trembling gladdies are raised – 'wave that glad, grab life by the stalk' – Edna celebrates her wonderfully mad, priapic ritual of benediction and renewal. This is the spirit of comedy at its oldest and best. When, after locking Edna in her dressing room, Barry Humphries himself returns in tux and black hat to take the final ovation, it is thrilling. He makes half a century's art look so easy we almost forget how extraordinary he is.

Wise Blood

Nick Cave and the Bad Seeds. Thebarton Theatre, December 1994.

More first feature than support act, Dave Graney and the Coral Snakes are having one of their lives. At Thebarton, most of the full-house crowd are inside to see them. The hypnotic sound of the Confessions of Gainsbourg surges into the Graney signature, *You're Too Hip For Me Baby.* Dave is the usual triumph of man-made fibre, doing his tai-chic workout while the band goes about its reliable business. Under blood-red lights Graney sings *You Wanna Be There But You Don't Wanna Travel.* Robin Casinader's keyboards chime above a murky sound mix. The foldback is obviously fine – Graney is gliding confidently, oblivious to the fact that bassist Gordy Blair is trapped inside a forty gallon drum.

The band work through the list – *Warren Oates*, *Won't You Ride With Me*, and the enticing repetitions of *There Was a Time*. Then Dave starts his attenuated Australian Doors joke. The ironists get it but this is a mixed crowd and you wonder whether maybe some of the Cave people think that even a channelling tribute band is better than no Jim at all. Just to add to the ambiguity, Dave curls his lip around *It's Your Crowd I Hate* before opening into the final cluster – *You Wanna Be Loved*, his classic Beat lyric, *Night of the Wolverine*, *The Stars, Baby, The Stars* and *I'm Gonna Release Your Soul*. The crowd roars, and the Coral Snakes look pleased even though we missed out on most of Rod Hayward's guitar. It has been good Graney all the same. There are no encores. The order of service is tight.

It's time for Saint Nick. And where else but Thebarton Theatre on an Adelaide Sunday evening would you look for the laying on of tongues, for the snake-handling pentecost of Nick Cave and the Bad Seeds. This is the Night of the Hunter, rock and roll Apocrypha. This, as the Ass said to the Angel, is Revelation. The backcloth announces the band's name – in blotchy blown-up type. I'm told that this favoured graphic of the underground press is currently available as a computer font. Smudgy Remington is now known as American Typewriter.

Through the reds and blues of the dim stage the band take their places. Thomas Wydler in back on the drums; Martyn Casey on bass; Conway Savage ready at the keyboard to transmit through hair and fingertips. Group linchpin, Mick Harvey, on guitar and synth, surveys the crowd from the OP side while guest Seed Jim Sclavunos gets ready to do some Roland Wolf.

Through the metallic, rippling keyboard chords – reminiscent of Barry Reynolds' arrangements for Marianne Faithfull's *Broken English* – comes Nick Cave, a stovepipe Rimbaud in a stovepipe suit. Cave swings his hank of dark hair. A lot has happened since we were last in Adelaide, he gruffly observes while the crowd goes palpable at the sheer idea of seeing the living ledge. A guy near me, stripped to the waist, is about to give himself an aneurysm bellowing his approval. One lung has punctured and the other one is flickering. His thorax and voice box unequal to the level of homage he has in mind, he switches from bellowing to a tinnitus-inducing whistle.

We are all enveloped – the old, the young, the halt, the lame, the lupine whistlers. Between the slicing piano and the hypnotic synth chords, between the essence and the descent comes – 'I found her on a night of fire and noise/wild bells rang in a wild sky ...' The portentous opening lines of what may yet be Cave's greatest song – *Do You Love Me*. Like the rest of *Let Love In*, Nick Cave's current album, it is galvanising proof that the singer is, to coin a phrase, at the height of his powers. He is certainly at the height of something – his audacity, his mythology as a post-punk, post-Berlin cult fave, his triumph over chemistry. Here is the man who survived his own birthday party.

It is hardly new to say that Nick Cave is a confluence of the Romantic Gothic. But it is worth noting yet again how well he does it. His imagery is derived from the Old Testament and the mad bits from Blake. The devotion to dark ladies is Petrarchan, with all the gallantry of Nosferatu. We have heard these hoarse, erotically languid vocals before. Leonard Cohen's S-and-M Sisters of Mercy for one, and James Morrison – before The End – said it all so prematurely. But neither Cohen nor the Doors at their overblown, legendary best could work a crowd with Cave's atavism. Like Flannery O'Connor's preacher from the Church with no Christ, Nick Cave has wise blood.

The Bad Seeds need no time to get bedded in. From the opening salvos they are in full cry, creating the hurricane of sound needed for the still centre of Cave's demonic intimacies – 'Do you love me, do you love me, do you love me?' And then, insinuating the unspeakable – 'Do you love me – LIKE I LOVE YOU ...' The playlist is well-rehearsed with no frigging around between numbers. There's the quirkily Appalachian-sounding, *Papa Won't Leave You Henry*, then the shunting rhythm and sudden eruptions of *Red Right Hand*. And, from the classic repertoire, *The Good Son*. One more man is … gone. Certainly, next to me, Whistler is near dementia with adulation. Fingers sprouting from his mouth he is surely summoning every dog from here to Semaphore. Asked by the now hearing-challenged around him if all this is entirely necessary, he explains that he wants to hear himself on the live recording. Now who will be the witness/When the fog's too thick to see?

Let Love In is well represented – the flesh tearing cadences of *Loverman* and, the title track itself, Cave's croony baritone somewhere between Johnny Cash and Graham Parker. Then the slow march chords of *The Ship Song* have the audience spell-bound as Cave offers rest to the weary and the Bad Seeds crank up every available keyboard. Chorus vocals come from Mick Harvey, Sclavunos and Blixa Bargeld, former engine of the German avant-garde band Einsturzende Neubauten. But any state of grace is temporary. *City of Refuge* and *Jack the Ripper* are taken to new intensities, the crowd to perilous levels of arousal.

And then lamentation. Go son, go down to the water. This is a weeping song, a song in which to weep. Again the drums and voices of the Bad Seeds create mass hypnosis. The solemnity of the song verges on the parodic. A flake like Jim Morrison couldn't have carried this one. Nick Cave knows the drama of the liturgy, the pathos of repetition. Skinny gremlin that he is, he drapes his arm around the melancholy statue of Blixa Bargeld, pale valkyrie, punk child of Schiller.

Jangling Jack gets the treatment but despite its catchy hook it is rather B grade stuff. Unlike *The Mercy Seat*. The band play in such alchemic unison they are like a great steel drum. The ringing hammers of the younger Blixa are reintegrated into a rock sound of ego-melting proportions. The Periodic Table of Elements is acquiring a new entry.

The sinuous ironies and cowboy strains of *Nobody's Baby Now* serve as first encore leaving us unguarded against the finale. *From Her to Eternity*. A six minute blitzkrieg, shades of David Byrne but with many more ergs. Atop Casey's pulsing bass and

Wydler's kettledrum, Cave croaks his circling lyrics while Blixa punctuates with shrieks, Conway Savage chops at the keyboard and various guitars angle-grind into perfect chaos.

After seventy one minutes Nick Cave and the Bad Seeds leave the stage and don't return. They play with such precision and intelligence you wonder what it would be like if they ambled a bit, Nick doing some talking, reading some poems – that kind of thing. There is something arm's length about this, American Typewriter, over-calibrated. Although not for the Whistler, who is now, as far as I can tell, nearly unconscious, his eyeballs have rolled back, his whistle fingers limp at his sides. He's either just been exorcised or he needs one. As for me, seventy-one minutes is just fine. I feel like my brains have been arc-welded. Any more and things could get Faustian.

The Memory of Other Minds: Remembering Babylon

David Malouf Chatto & Windus/Random House $29.95 (hb)
Editions, June, 1993, pp. 21–2

Despite their apparent diversity of subject and setting David Malouf's novels all seem to circle back to questions of the imagination and the way it is triggered by language. As a poet Malouf has the plainest belief in the naming of things, a capacity that is so essential to the characters in his novels that it literally saves their wits. In *Fly Away Peter*, Jim Saddler's fastidiously ordered observations of the topography and birdlife of the Queensland swamplands are carried as a kind of mental ballast as he is drawn towards extinction in the trenches of France.

His friend Ashley Crowther recognises Saddler's deep connection to territory:

> Such claims were ancient and deep. They lay in Jim's knowledge of every blade of grass and drop of water in the swamp, of every bird's foot that was set down there; in his having a vision of the place and the power to give that vision breath; in his having, most of all, the names for things and in that

> way of possessing them. It went beyond mere convention or the law.

This capacity to reconstruct, to call up elaborate mnemonics, is quite precisely explored in Malouf's short autobiographical work *12 Edmondstone Street:*

> The house is a field of dense affinities, laid down, each one, with an almost physical power, in the life we share with all that in being `familiar' has become essential to us, inseparable from what we are. We are drawn back magically, magnetically, to our own sticky fingerprints. Even in their ghostly state, on objects long since dispersed. They haunt us. Set loose in a world of things, we are struck at first by their terrible otherness. It drives us to fury. For a time we are all mouth, we try to swallow them, then to smash them to smithereens – little hunters on the track of the ungraspable. Till we perceive at last that in naming and handling things we have power over them. If they refuse to yield their history to us they may at least, in time, become agents in ours. This is the process of our first and deepest education.

The power to recall is seen as restorative, indeed crucial, to Digger and Vic drawn into *The Great World* and its war. In the terrible conditions of Changi prison Digger travels like a shaman on the viewless wings of recollection when his friend Mac describes his house in Sydney and he visualises it room by room:

> In the dark while the house slept, he waited quietly in the kitchen, his spirit touched by the light off those plates, in his hands the dryness of a bit of stale bread ... Once, standing there he heard a movement behind him and Iris came in in her nightgown. She didn't see him of course. She walked right past him to a sink, took a glass, filled it with water from the tap and drank, very slowly gazing into the dark yard. He watched her as if the ordinary act was miraculous. It was miraculous. It slaked his thirst.

It is the discovery of such auguries of innocence, catalogues of commonplace reality that offers balm to the abraded minds of the Changi captives:

> Memory was a gift, when they really set themselves to it. Lists. You started one and it could be extended forever, back and back, and gone over endlessly, and what you called up became a magic formula for keeping yourself in the world or for wiping yourself, temporarily, out of it. For some it was the numbers game. What they went back to was the number plates of various cars they owned or had driven at times for the firms they worked for. These numbers were it. Got into the right order, like the combination of a safe they were a key that would unlock the universe. For others it was railway stations. The stations for instance from Redfern on the Western Line. They went through them slowly, in morning heat sometimes but at others in the chill of smoky winter, on their way to work.

In *An Imaginary Life*, in many respects still the central text in Malouf's work, the author identifies deeply with the exiled Ovid, poet without language, namer without referents:

> They are not uncivil. But no one in Tomis speaks my tongue, and for nearly a year now I have heard no word of my own language; I am rendered dumb. I communicate like a child with grunts and signs, I point, I raise my eyebrows questioning, I burst into tears of joys if someone-a child even – understands what I am trying to say. In the open I go about shouting, talking to myself simply to keep the words in my head, or drive them out of it.

The poet, like Jim Saddler or the Changi inmates, finds abundance in privation, intensity undreamed of in the voluble urbanity of his former life. When he finds a wild poppy it releases a stream of imaginative ecstasy:

> A little wild poppy, of a red so sudden it made my blood stop. I kept saying the word over and over to myself, scarlet, as if the

> word, like the colour, had escaped me till now, and just saying it would keep the little windblown flower in sight. Poppy. The magic of saying the word made my skin prickle, the saying almost a greater miracle than seeing ... Poppy, scarlet poppy, child of my far-off childhood and the cornfields round our farm at Sulmo, I have brought you into being, I have raised you out of my earliest memories, out of my blood, to set you blowing in the winds. Scarlet. Magic word on the tongue to flash again on the eye. Scarlet. And with it all the other colours come flooding back, as magic syllables, and the earth explodes with them, they flash about me. I am making the spring.

For the silvery tongued Ovid this struggle for expression brings renewed reverence for the primitive business of naming. When the wolf boy is brought to his village it is the rough, practical dialect of Tomis – only recently acquired by the poet himself – that Ovid chooses to teach him. In return the Child of nature teaches him, like Caliban, all the qualities of the isle, the fresh springs, brine pits, barren place and fertile.

An Imaginary Life is a poet's journey, a dense Romantic lyric in praise of the numinous in the nature. The Child becomes father to the man, companion and guide to the edge of what is revealed as an Arcadian world. It is an extraordinarily harmonious work and for that reason remains Malouf's most thoroughly satisfying one.

Remembering Babylon, his latest novel, bears strong structural resemblances to An Imaginary Life but has a courage and a sense of risk that makes it even more admirable. With each new work, it seems, comes greater acuity and confidence. In *The Great World*, with its focus on that part of Australian male culture which found apotheosis in wartime, David Malouf brought freshness to a subject in danger of being done to death. With Reme*mbering Babylon* he examines the vexed matter of European settlement in colonial Queensland, the attempts to embrace the new world and the violence of denial.

His narrative begins with deconstructive abruptness:

> One day in the middle of the nineteenth century, when settlement in Queensland had advanced little more than halfway up the coast, three children were playing at the edge of a paddock when they saw something extraordinary.

Malouf's fable is about Gemmy Fairlie, a London urchin who has escaped his servitude to the Dickensian rogue Willett and jumped ship. Cast off along the Queensland coast, delirious, disturbed and a mere thirteen he is taken in by a party of blacks with whom he lives for the next sixteen years. He reappears to the settlers, a raggedy apparition with the merest fragments of English – 'Do not shoot,' he shouts at the children Lachlan Beattie and Janet McIvor, 'I'm a British object.'

The accidental truth of his solecism – which Malouf found mentioned in a contemporary document – is expanded and explored in Remembering Babylon. Like An Imaginary Life its structure is historical, but its texture and insight has, as the author puts it, no origin in fact. Its truth, of course, is quite another matter. The circumstance of a child of nature returning to society has immediate echoes of the Wild Boy of Aveyron, a source for *An Imaginary Life*. It also suggests the case of Kasper Hauser, the youth found in a town square in Germany after spending his whole life in an attic. Flourishing at great pace after such arrested development, Hauser, like Victor in Itard's story of the Aveyron boy and Ovid's Child, was an embodiment of the virtue of education, a humanist parable of the cultivation of the mind.

Interestingly, in his newest book Malouf subverts this satisfaction. Instead, Gemmy remains a dangling man with remnants of his European past and inarticulate wisdom from his Aboriginal reality. There is none of Greystoke's suave return to society, none of Kasper Hauser's literary acumen. This is not a happy fable of the enlightened return. Gemmy's inner life remains opaque and he becomes a kind of Rorschach test for a community stretched to twanging on a continuum from hatred to bewildered concern.

Using an epigraph from Blake – 'Whether this is Jerusalem or Babylon we know not' – Malouf examines the settlers' reaction to a new land and an unfathomable indigenous population:

> Most unnerving of all was the knowledge that, just three years back, the very patch of earth you were standing on had itself been on the other side of things, part of the unknown, and might still, for all your coming and going over it, and the sweat you had poured into its acre or two of ploughed earth, have the last mystery upon it, in jungle brakes between paddocks and ferny places out of the sun. Good reason, that, for stripping it, as soon as you could manage, of every vestige of the native; for ringbarking and clearing and reducing it to what would make it, at last, just a bit like home.

But not all want to transform the world, some are transformed by it. There is Gemmy of course. When he learns a new language it is, as with the Child in *An Imaginary Life*, a whole new grammar of living:

> What kept you alive here was the one and the other, and they were inseparable: the creature with its pale ears raised and stiffened, sitting up alert in its life as you were in yours, and its name on your tongue. When it kicked its feet and gushed blood it did not go out of the world but had its life now in you, and could go in and out of your mouth for ever, breath on breath, and was not lost, nay more than the water you stooped to drink would cease to run because you gulped it down in greedy mouthfuls, then pissed it out.
>
> Young enough to learn and to be shaped as if for the first time, he was young enough also to forget. he lost his old language in the new one that came to his lips. He had never in fact possessed more than the few hundred words that were immediately needful to him, to fill his belly or save his skin ... As for things, nothing he had dealt with had been his own. He stammered over most of them, b-b-boots, j-j-jug; his hold was buttery. Now they slipped away altogether, they

> dropped out of life, and with them, and the words whatever thin threads had held them together and made up the fabric of his world.

Gemmy is not completely converted to his new world though. When he hears the storytelling of his magical arrival to his new Aboriginal family:

> He would listen, and in one part of himself, the part that belonged to their tribal life, he believed, but in some other part he did not. There was a different story, he thought, which was alone and secret: which had another shape, and might need, for its telling, the words he had had in his mouth when they first found him, and had lost: though not, he thought forever.

Just as Gemmy has the shadow of memory of another life, so do those who are drawn towards him. Frazer, the minister, for instance, carries with him the spirit of nineteenth century botanical study. His painstaking specimen paintings, his project for hybridising native fruits and his halting attempts to learn Gemmy's lore and dialect show him a man capable of worshipping more than one god. George Abbot, the prim young schoolteacher who carries words of French as totems against the unknown, is enriched by the new age salon presided over by Mrs Hutchence, a beneficent nature mystic who functions very like a character such as Emerson in Forster's *A Room With a View*. It is Mrs Hutchence who teaches the young Janet McIvor the principles of beekeeping but it is Gemmy who is her spirit guide when she is overpowered by a swarm.

Even the practical, battling McIvor family is altered by the presence of Gemmy Fairlie. Jock McIvor is forced to choose between the redneck viciousness of his neighbours or stand by the disconcerting changeling who is sheltering under his roof. But as with the others, in naming the other in himself he is released.

Malouf doesn't trade in glib mysticism. *Remembering Babylon* powerfully evokes the vengeance of puritanism, and everywhere the shadow of the known facts of European contact with Aboriginals quickens the sense of a road not taken. In a crucial incident, when Gemmy is visited by two blacks in full view of the community, Malouf gives a glimpse of the animistic richness of the white blackfella's life:

> [The blacks] were concerned that in coming here, among these ghostly white creatures, he might have slipped back into the thinner world of wraiths and demons that he has escaped, though never completely, in his days with them. They had come to reclaim: but lightly, bringing what would feed his spirit.
>
> They spread out the land for him, gave him its waters to drink. As he took huge draughts, saw it light his flesh. Watched him, laughing, bathe in it, scooping great handfuls over his breast. In the little space of dust between them as they sat, they danced, beat up clouds, threw rainbows over their heads. Then they rose, exchanged the formalities of parting and went.

That Babylon might really be Jerusalem is not a suggestion from the forked tongue of babel nor a fanciful meditation on the noble savage. David Malouf's splendid new novel further elaborates the immanence and energy of ordinary things – something known better by some Australians than others and of greater value to some than others. Far from being a comfortable homily *Remembering Babylon* is a sometimes difficult and unresolved book, an intense, quirky narrative made up of shards of recognition and glimpses of disparate characters momentarily experiencing epiphanies of shared being. It is a book to be savoured, a memory of our own memories.

Malaysia, Santorini and Beyond …

KIRPAL SINGH
SINGAPORE UNIVERSITY OF MANAGEMENT

Before you taught me to be an oenophile
You taught me travel
On a Malaysian balcony with Jane
Could only happen once –
You never felt good with repeats

Your keen mind with that cutting wit
Which so struck me from the very first
Moved many in different ways, even to tears
Amidst the frolicking and the cavorting
And the lies and the shams and the shandies

You always choose the best, the original
Routes, roots and rude awakenings
Like how you pissed in the diplomat's garden
Saw him cower beneath your towering grin
And then apologised like a good gentleman!

On that eventful nite when you insisted
I drank before returning home–
My tee totalling years were going to end –
We finished 13 bottles and were still talking
When good Jane left for school the next morning
And the birds in your valley had flown
And our brains had been verily touched by wine

In vino veritas, that old motto you flourished.

The good years have rushed us by, Syd
In age we see others faltering yet strong
Because they, unlike us, haven't drunk so much
Nor indulged nor known the cunning
Of human hearts wronged and violated
Clinging to positions, functioning at best
To prompts and pre-emptives and subtle insinuation.

Seeing Jaime turn cricket into manhood
I recall the splendour of KI, the jetty
Where so much caroused and our memories
Taking refuge in the exploits of pristine sands
Connecting history with fiction with force.

Foregrounding Ada to Lolita you preferred
That delicate personal touch of honest sharing
Which your students still recount with relish
And the wonder of your curious probing
Opening new worlds to these young
Seeking glories in literature and self.

All is now changed my friend –
Books, pedagogies, frames for referencing
Dense coded vocabularies now trample
The old honesties as we fumble understanding
And track our savannahs across the skies.

But somewhere, as always, you beckon
That twinkle which so seduced all
Now testimony to a new glory, a new eye
Still sparkling the way forward
Along with the lapses surrounding us.

The Darville/Demidenko Affair: Jew and anti-Jew in Australian Fiction

RON SHAPIRO
UNIVERSITY OF WESTERN AUSTRALIA

Now that the recent Helen Darville/Demidenko debate had had some time to cool off – at least the 'story' is no longer prominent on the front page of the national daily newspapers – it is perhaps worth reminding ourselves of several things. First we need to be aware of past representations of the Jewish stereotype over the course of Australian literary history. For this is by no means the first time anti-Jewish literary representations have occurred in Australian literature, or that anti-Jewish literary representations have passed muster unobserved or else misunderstood, by readers and literary critics. Second it is well worth pondering the kind of authorial moral neutrality which is to be associated with our postmodernist era, something which I think will help account for the curious public response to the novel.

Australia inherited most of its narrow racial assumptions from Britain where the figure of the stereotypic Jew can be traced back to the beginnings of British civilisation. The representation of Jewish character in *The Hand that Signed the Paper* falls squarely into a long-established British and European pattern of anti-Jewish imagery which saw the Jew as the model of international conspirator, the cabbalist, the mastermind whose intelligence posed a threat to society. Those allegedly Bolshevist Jews who were supposed to be responsible for crimes against Ukranians and so deserved what they got in the Holocaust at the hands of Hitler's SS constitute a single variation on an already larger long-established theme. What distinguishes the stereotype of the Jew in the Western world from a multitude of other equally pernicious stereotypes is its antiquity – it goes back at least to King Herod who may be regarded as the archetype from the myth of the Middle Ages of the Jew as child-killer and aspiring Christ killer. Chaucer and Shakespeare inherited European anti-Jewishness since they constructed their Jewish stereotypes in a period when Jews had been banished from England, and it can be argued that the very absence of the actual Jewish presence in England at that time helped foster a more grotesque symbolic anti-human caricature. In Shylock the twin myths of Jews as killers of Christians and as legalistically minded usurers were combined in the imagery of the knife and pound of flesh, not to forget the additional suggestion of the human heart as offal and the possibility of Jewish cannibalism. Marlowe's Jew, Barabas is equally the poisoner of wells, the charge laid against Jews that it was they who were responsible for the Black Plague of Europe. The early literary representation of the Jew is thus the stereotype of the devil and the demon; as sorcerer, blasphemer, and ritual murderer; as desecrator and heretic; as usurer and infidel – the full panoply of the 'Devil's own'[1]. Researching this subject during the Second World War, Joshua Trachtenberg noted the immediate correspondence between this medieval caricature and Hitler's portrait of the dirty malformed Jew in *Mein Kempf* and the hunch-backed bird-beaked cartoon-like creatures who are the subject of the anti-Jewish forgery *The Protocols of the Elders of Zion*, a book which since the war and even in more recent times had helped internationally to shape notions as far afield ad Arabia and Japan as to what he essential Jew, and accordingly also the Israeli, really is.

One of the interesting points to have emerged from the recent Demidenko affair is just how many highly literate educated Australians, including some of this country's leading academics and writers, repeatedly fail to recognise anti-Jewishness even when it is staring them in the face (and I intend using the term 'anti-Jewishness' in this paper instead of the more commonly inaccurate 'anti-Semitism' which would literally have to include all Arabic peoples). The Vogel Judges' Report praises the Darville/Demidenko novel for breaking new ground and as a 'multi-voiced novel of shifting perspectives'[2], words suggesting the kind of democratic polyvocality which most of us would like to associate with the new Australian multiculturalism (despite the irony that in the novel most of these many voices come from the same single side). On the novel's back cover David Marr speaks of this 'astonishingly talented' writer, and Jill Kitson finds in the book 'a searingly truthful account of terrible wartime deeds that is also an imaginative work of extraordinary redemptive power' (which whatever exactly this means, sound suspiciously evangelical to my ears). I am not arguing that these and many similar claims couched in similarly euphoric, and somehow strangely empty, language are necessarily wrong. They perhaps reflect the contemporary postmodern spirit. But one is struck by the absence of an accompanying awareness of the sort of problems a novel like this raises, and an equal absence of the hoary tradition of anti-Jewish scapegoating. Margaret Jones of the *Sydney Morning Herald*, offered the admission that 'it did not occur to me that the book was, as some critics have suggested, loathsomely anti-Semitic' but 'now that all the warning signals have gone up, even, a non-Jewish reader can see how it is possible to read anti-Semitism into it. The real point is that this novel allows itself to be read in whichever way one likes, thus reflecting its author's allegiance to the principle of postmodernist neutrality. The first half of this paper will attempt to address, however, briefly, the manner of representation of the Jew in past Australian fiction and society; in the second half I shall try to pick up some threads in so far as they have some bearing on *The Hand that Signed the Paper*.

At the time of the arrival of the First Fleet, Australia inherited a literary and poetic tradition of anti-Jewishness from Britain almost two hundred years following the British institutionalisation of anti-Jewishness in stage characters like Shylock and

Barabas. Theoretical or symbolic anti-Jewishness is reflected in the colonial Australian literature in the common or generic designation 'the Jew', for instance occurring in the stories of John George Lang who was Australia's first writer of fiction in the mid-nineteenth century (who incidentally himself had a convict Jewish grandfather who landed with the First Fleet). In the mid-nineteenth century Australia the stereotype of the Jew was far more widely familiar in the general population than in the second half of the twentieth. What is of special interest in John Lang's colonial fictional thriller *The Forger's Wife* is that actual Jewishness, where it matters, is disguised beneath a Gentile name. The novel's main character, a detective called George Flower, was based on Sydney's most famous policeman of the 1820s and 30s, Israel Chapman. George Flower is an interesting character who as Nancy Keesing has said, rises above the general melodrama of Lang's story,[4] a character who operates ambiguously on both sides of the law as a 'thief taker' employing methods almost as crooked as those of the crooks – for Israel Chapman was, it seems, a kind of Australian Jewish colonial Mike Hammer. And while Chapman's Jewish identity in Lang's story is disguised (no doubt for the sake of greater acceptability) another relatively minor character, a publican by profession, is simply designated 'the Jew'. And it seems that there was a similar concealment of the true name of the Jewish protagonist in James Tucker's convict novel *Ralph Rashleigh* written sometime in the 1840s in which the protagonist's adversary at one point in the book is a ruthless penal officer, an overseer of institutionalised convicts, a man described as 'a small, stunted abortion of humanity[5] who appears to be seen as an example of his wicked Jewish tribe. But on occasion, as in Alexander Harris' *The Emigrant Family* (1849), the Jew and Jewess are treated far more liberally, though the author makes it quite clear that there is nothing at all that can reverse the historical mistake and salve the Jews' sadness 'that our unhappy nation should have crucified the Good One.'[6]

But it is towards the end of the nineteenth century with the rise of Australian nationalism that anti-Jewishness and a more general xenophobia took on a special social and cultural significance. The more nationalistic often meant, among writers like Henry Lawson and Marcus Clarke, the more anti-Jewish. Clarke, author of the humanist novel *For the Term of His Natural Life* was known 'to sustain a campaign of anti-Jewish sneers and references,' and as a man for whom all Jewry represented 'a huge bank which keeps the table against all Christendom'? In his short story 'Gentleman George's Bride,' the crooked businessman Mr Israel Davis admits to a Jewish world conspiracy:

> We are all connected: we all help each other. Do you ever see a Jew dig or beg, or do menial service? Did you ever have a Jew servant? Did you ever know a Jew, however poor, who hadn't a sovereign to lend at interest? My dear sir, we Jews rule the world. When we were turned out of ... Jerusalem, we made a vow to take possession of the Universe – and we've done it too.[8]

Then there is Joseph Furphy's philosophical pipe-smoking Tom Collins in *Such is Life* and *Rigby's Romance*. Julian Croft notes that in Furphy's writing Jews are portrayed as whining malcontents, who resist change and challenge, and at every opportunity fall back on their idolatrous ways. Or Du Maurier's play *Trilby* (mentioned as a passing reference in Miles Franklin's *My Brilliant Career*), a story about an evil-minded, dirty fingered hypnotising Jew, which was shown in Australia in 1895 and proved a huge success with Australian audiences. And the Sydney *Bulletin*, so often celebrated for its championing of early Australian fiction, was just one of many journals and newspapers of the period which were generally xenophobic and specifically rabidly anti-Jewish – in the case of the *Bulletin* right up to the 1960s. At the lower end of the journalistic scale the editor of the Sydney Truth could write in 1905:

> Theologically, ethnologically, ethno-psychologically, ethno-technically, and it might almost be said, anthropologically, the Jews are anti-pathetic if not absolutely antagonistic to the great civilised comity of Christian nations of the West.[10]

Louis Stone in his well-known novel *Jonah* (1911) capitalised on the Jewish stereotype in his portrait of the larrikin leader of a Sydney street-gang whose sly intelligence eventually takes him from rags to riches:

> a hunch-back, with the uncanny look of the deformed – the head, large and powerful, wedged between shoulders as if a giant's hand had pressed it down, the hump projecting behind, monstrous and inhuman. His face held you with a pair of restless grey eyes, the colour and temper of steel, deep with malicious intelligence. His nose was large and thin, curved like the beak of an eagle.[11]

Here are all the gross physical deformities combined with the suggestion of cold humanity together with the malicious intelligence in a creature who is 'as crafty ad a the devil'[12] and who 'had an eye for business like a Jew'.[13] It is interesting that Stone is strangely cautious, like Lang, about making the Jewish identity totally explicit but in this case employs a familiar mode of insinuation through simile which enhances the suggestion of the Jew's craftiness and the way he operates through deceit and disguise. Jonah as a shrewd businessman is not so much a surprising Jewish representation as Jonah the street-gang leader. Yet there are historical examples of the way young Jews were sometimes falsely taken to be street hoodlums,[14] and quite probably this was partly a carry-over from the nineteenth century British experience of the poor Jews of East London and criminals like Dickens fictional Fagin and Bill Sykes; in fact Dicken's Fagin was based on Ikey Solomon who was among the earliest transported to Australia.

But far more surprising than Louis Stone's representation of the transformation of this Australian larrikin from petty criminal to successful businessman is the response of several generations of Australian literary critics, who, almost to a person, have wholly failed to recognise a glaringly anti-Jewish stereotype standing at the head of our literary tradition. Yet as astute and Australianist as Dorothy Green in her 1965 essay on Jonah continues the Australian custom of missing the anti-Jewish wood for the obvious trees. After noting in the character Jonah, for instance 'some affinity with the Biblical character of the same name', she goes on to ask the central question, a question she argues that almost everyone had thus far totally overlooked: 'Why ... does Stone,' she asks, 'repeat several times, like a theme tune, the exact terms of his physical description of Jonah?'[15] And her answer is wonderfully bathetic: she simply offers a kind of Freudian interpretation of Jonah's physical features which somehow, she argues, proves that Louis Stone suffered from a neglected childhood.

Strangely, there is comfort as well as concern to be taken from this kind of Australian naivety: namely that it reflects the relative absence of real everyday anti-Jewishness in Australian society, especially when compared with most European countries over the greater course of this century. Interesting too, especially in view of Stone's close relationship with the notably anti-Jewish Norman Lindsay, is the possibility that Stone himself disguised some personal Jewish family connection.

Apart from the wonderful stories of Russian immigrant writer Solomon Stedman in the early 1930s it wasn't until the late 30s and 40s with the new wave of immigrants from eastern Europe that Jewish authors like Pinchas Goldhar, Hertz Bergner and Judah Waten started to speak in a distinctively Jewish voice and to 'write back' to correct older anti-Jewish stereotypes. In the period between Louis Stone's Jonah and the more authentic Jewish voice flourished a range of popular novels featuring Jews in their most ancient and stereotypic roles. For instance there wad H.M. Abbott who wrote a novel *Castle Vane: A Romance of Bushranging on the Upper Hunter in the Olden Days* (1920), the olden days referring to the 1840s and the particular historical circumstance none other than the episode of bush-ranging and cattle-duffing which was historically based on a real-life bush-ranger, Edward Davis, known as Teddy the Jew Boy. Starting from a meagre historical account of Edward Davis's bush-ranging exploits in NSW in the 1840s, Abbott used the opportunity to exploit the mythology of a Jewish world conspiracy. In his novel (which follows the Fagin and Bill Sykes formula) the bent bearded Jew, Jacob Losky, is (predictably enough) a book and antique dealer who runs a Sydney bookshop. But (equally predictably) the bookshop is just a front for recruiting men pursued by the law into New South Wales bushranging operation. The old Jew is really 'a master craftsman in crime'[16] who masterminds the gang run by his younger co-religionist who has adopted the actual historical name of Edward Davis but is better known throughout the neighbourhood as 'Teddy the Jew Boy', a man with the character of a tormented Heathcliff. And to complete the nest of stereotypes there is Jacob Losky's far too beautiful Jewish grand-daughter Rachel, a Jessica type, the kind of Jewish temptress Sartre once, talking about the far-too-beautiful Jewish daughter stereotype, described as 'emana[ting for an anti-Semite] a subtle odour of rape and massacre'[17]. The message is clear: not only were larrikinism and mercantilism in Australia in the 19th century to be attributed to Jews of the likes of Jonah, but bushranging and harlotry too, it seem, were also part of the larger Jewish conspiracy which, as we saw earlier in the case of Tucker's *Ralph Rashleigh*, was also involved in the running of Australia's penal settlements. Abbott's novel was published in 1920, a period of profound anti-nationalism and xenophobia which followed the First World War, and the novel represents an interesting instance of the de-glamorising of what formerly throughout the nineteenth century from Edward Davis to Ned Kelly had been very glamorised Australian colonial bushranging mythology. Also published in 1920 was Aidan de Brune's popular whodunit *The Shadow Crook* which further demonstrated that some of Australia's greatest company frauds in the gold and pearling industries of northern Australia were the work of lecherous Jews like de Brune's shadowy fictional character Abel Minto, alias, Samuel Keene.[18]

The 1920s were also a period in which conservative forces within Australia were bent on showing their opposition to the new Modernism which they saw as a serious threat to the conventional Western aesthetic. Specifically the dangers were pinpointed as 'black culture Jazz and Cubism) and Jewish wealth and taste'. The magazine Vision which started in 1923 regarded modernism as 'a direct assault by charlatans and Jews on the finest traditions of Western art'.[19] And as late as 1941 P.R. Stephensen 'could still rage … against modernism as decadent Jewish mysticism'.[20] Of course this was fiction and scare-mongering and we might expect fiction to be far-fetched. Except, that is, when reality (or at least what purports to be reality) is stranger than fiction, as was the case of a certain British anthropologist in the mid-nineteenth century, Henry Ansell, who claimed that certain tribes of Australian Aborigines, particularly in Western Australia, were in fact Jews, the lost tribes of Israel as also were all the Papuan people to Australia's north. As evidence to support these claims this anthropologist cited his findings that these illiterate Australian tribes 'never hut on Saturdays', 'abhor pork, and only eat fish with fins and scales', and 'when shown a Hebrew prayer book recognised several passages in it.'[21]

A good deal has been written about the Australian reaction to European refugees or 'refujews' seeking entry into Australia around the time of the Second World War. There is the well-known instance of the Dunera boys who were impounded because they spoke Yiddish and German. Jews were suspected of being Nazi spies,[22] as was anyone speaking a foreign language (this Australian suspicion of all foreigners was a virtual repeat of the situation of the First World War, memorably presented for example in Judah Waten's retrospective novel *The Unbending* (1954)).In 1940 the Australian government banned all telephone conservations which were not conducted in English – though French could be spoken by special permission.[23] Even Australia's established Anglo-Jewry was afraid that an influx of European Jews would arouse Australian hostilities. New refugees were told in no uncertain terms by a CIB agent at a massed assembly in Sydney in 1939 how they should behave, or rather how they should not behave in Australia, instructions supported by Australia's Anglo-Jewry:

> Don't barter or haggle over prices. Avoid making yourself conspicuous by your manner and dress. Those flat leather portfolios you carry, those over-coats reaching nearly to the ground may be fashionable in Europe, but in Australia it simply advertises the fact that you are a Jewish refugee.[24]

Jewish immigrants were accused of flouting industrial awards and undermining Australian working conditions. In 1939 the then President of the Victorian Legislative Council, Sir Frank Clarke, attacked the 'hundreds of weedy East Europeans ... slinking rat-faced men under five feet in height with a chest development of about twenty inches ... [who] worked in back-yard factories in Carlton and other localities north of Melbourne for two or three shillings a week pocket money and their keep'.[25]

What is always interesting to notice about Jewish and anti-Jewish writing is how opposite they are. Jewish writers of the 1940s onward deconstruct the anti-Jewish stereotype in no uncertain terms, even when not deliberately aiming to do so. The Yiddish and English stories of Goldhar, Bergner and Waten tap directly into the weighty Yiddish literary tradition of Eastern Europe in which Jews, although outwardly recognisable as 'types' constitute a varied and heterogeneous community of complex multi-faceted individuals, as notably to be found in the works of European authors like Kafka and Isaac and Israel Joshua Singer. One of the amazing and endearing qualities of Isaac Singer's novels, for instance, is the sheer range of different appearances, personalities and philosophies.

Moreover it has long been characteristic of Jewish writing to pull no punches, to describe Jews warts and all. In Solomon Stedman's Australian short story written in 1933 entitled 'My Neighbour's Story'[26] the Australian Jewish stereotype of the storekeeper/businessman is put under close critical scrutiny. Joe Pit and his alter-ego Joseph Pitkovsky, the new and old persona of one successful immigrant businessman, live their single life in mutual opposition to one another. What the shrewd stereotypical Joe Pit achieves in the way of success Joseph Pitkovksy despises, the material acquisitiveness which is Joe Pit's raison d'etre Joseph Pitkovsky regards as worthless in the larger view of things, and so on. In other words the Joe Pit stereotype is only the one face, the public, knowable, and yet the relatively unimportant side of this successful Jewish businessman. One is reminded of Henry Vander Sluice alias Roy Rene alias 'Mo'. Probably Australia's best loved comedian of the previous generation, who lived a double life of vulgar Jewish comedian on-stage and shy, prudish and rather fastidious family man off-stage.[27] Or else of the comments made by the once famous American jazz clarinetist of the 1930s, Arthur Jacob Arshawsky, who said that he could never ever quite work out who this strange Artie Shaw fellow really was.[28]

∞

Following the above brief survey, I want to angle the discussion back to my starting point and the Darville/Demidenko affair because although this might seem too sudden a shift, it is in part what the previous discussion has been leading up to. Perhaps the most significant point to emerge from a lot of recent heated debate over the multi-prize-winning book, and pertinent to the above discussion is how little the various judges and defenders of *The Hand that Signed the Paper* know about this age-old anti-Jewish stereotype in literature, let alone in Jewish history. I should say in quasi-parenthesis here that I am not altogether convinced that an anti-Jewish reading is the only possible reading, sine I suspect that this novel merely exploits the kind of structural amorality which is intrinsic to postmodernist modes of representation; any argument with the novel therefore (and there is plenty to argue about!) really involves other more insidious 'invisible' villains. But my point is that even if the novel does deserve the many accolades it has received one might have expected from the judges some indication of their awareness of the many complex issues, literary as well as historical, which this kind of novel raises. To speak in very simple terms of the book's valuable contribution to contemporary Australian multicultural writing, or else to say that it is the book itself rather than the author which is being judged merely side-steps many difficult but vitally important questions. The so-called New Criticism earlier this century valorised the book itself as embodying a kind of fixed aesthetic object which could be judged on its own terms, and in more recent times the excessive and cultish textualisation of literature with the influences of structuralism, post-structuralism, post-structuralism, postmodernism, etc., has in many ways tended to reinforce an essentially textual or aesthetic reading and conception of literature. On the other hand, Marxist, feminist, and post-colonialist readings have resisted aestheticisation and have tried (though not always successfully) to insist on the necessity of agency or the practical applicability of all ideology and insist on the complex social and linguistic codification of which all literary texts are primarily constituted.

While the academic arguments continue to be hammered out it seems to me that the more textual arguments have tended to commandeer the academic and official public debate as to how literature works (though probably not the attitude of the 'average' non-academic reader who still believes that literature speaks about an actual knowable world). The Darville/ Demidenko affair is perhaps a timely reminder that what the reading of literature involves us in is more than mere aesthetic bookishness. In recent philosophical study of aesthetics Anne Sheppard concludes:

> Works of art are not isolated from the artists who produce them, from the world which provides their material, or from the audience to whom they are presented. At the same time they do not stand in any simple and direct relationship to artist, world, or audience, since the artist's experiences and the material offered by the world are reshaped into an artistic form and the audience responds to the forma s well as the content of the work.[29]

What is urgently required is a more balanced view. To attempt to judge literature on 'literary merit alone' would be, I believe, to mistake literature for some quite fixed separate construction which has little to do with the way people's lives are actually lived, and I doubt whether this is actually the way any book is ever read or judged. Literature possesses its own inner workings, but it is also something which intersects at every possible human level with the experiences of the living and the dead, the semi-living and he semi-dead. The book itself argument cannot stand up to scrutiny. One wonders what the response of the judges would have been, for instance, if *The Hand that Signed the Paper* had been the manuscript submitted by a balding middle-aged man with a known Nazi past instead of an impetuous young 'multicultural' talent. It is hard to imagine that anyone in that case would have insisted on arguing either that the author and the author's past have no bearing on the book itself, or that the remarkable authorial neutrality and lack of intervention is something to be approved and applauded.

On the other hand this is only part of the necessarily fuller argument. Plato wanted the poets banned from his republic because he contended that fiction bends the truth. Fiction is empowered with the capacity to sway rational judgement to the extent that it engages our sympathies. What then of the story which may engage our attention even against our better judgement? It seems to me that this is the situation with a novel like *The Hand that Signed the Paper* that it demands we feel sympathetic for people to whom we would normally refuse all sympathy. No-one has yet satisfactorily answered the conundrum Plato posed. All fiction in a sense 'lies' so as to gain our interest and/or sympathies and understanding. All literature is inherently seductive, and so challenges our foundational ethical assumptions.

Yet I suggest that if there are no firm answers there are at least some guidelines. First, we must dispel the idea of a pure art form, and recognise that purity like all such conceptual categories can always be deconstructed, and that a novel is very likely to impact in very specific ways on specific people in specific times and places since it participates in social and community values and shared experiences. For some Jews *The Hand that Signed the Paper* will appear to reinstate a familiar variant on the old Jewish stereotype – this time the Jew exposed as Bolshevist sadist and murderer – are few and scattered and where they do exist they seem extraordinarily half-hearted, leaving little room for doubt that the Jews in the Ukraine were simply receiving their proper comeuppance. Second, it is sometimes hard to know who exactly is best qualified to pronounce adequately on any particular piece of art or literature. It is generally assumed, for instance, that anyone connected with the arts is qualified to write about or comment on the arts or to award prizes in the arts. But a novel like *The Hand that Signed the Paper* ought to make us more chary of this easy assumption. For if we dismiss the notion that art can wholly be judged on 'the work itself', the argument that I am proposing in this paper, then it would follow that this particular sort of novel demands a higher than normal level of expertise: at a minimum it would require a reasonable knowledge of the wider history of the relations between Ukrainians and Jews in that country in order to determine how this particular period of history is being represented and so to judge more accurately the implications arising from this particular example of representation – implications affecting not only matters such as the 'quality of writing' but also affecting the quality of actual contemporary human lives and memories of past lives.

While public attention regarding the matter of anti-Jewishness has rightly, for a variety of literary and non-literary reasons, been focused on the Darville/Demidenko novel, it also needs to be pointed out that the stereotypical Jew can be seen to live on in a number of other contemporary Australian works. While accepting that the use of a caricature and reduction/enlargement as an age-old literary tool, I contend that we need to be far more aware – more aware than we are at present – of the kind of stereotypical representations which still occur, and with greater frequency than might imagine. One might point, for instance, to Brian Castro's parody of a Jew, Abraham Feingold, in *Birds of Passage* (1980), a mindless businessman characterised by his thick broken Yiddish accent and an obsession for money – all the odder in a novel devoted to the deconstruction of stereotypes – in this novel the stereotype of the Chinaman. One is reminded of Ruth Park's novel *The Harp in the South* (1948) and of the sharp-beaked Joseph Mendel, together with his deformed and licentious nephew Tommy Mendel; for while Ruth park was anxious to expose the popular stereotypes of her day such as popular representations of the Irish and the dwarf, she had few qualms, it appears, regarding this kind of outrageous Mendel caricature. Or one might ask, in the case of Jean Bedford's impressive novel *Sister Kate* (1982), what lies behind the character Aaron Sherrit, a man represented as the Judas Iscariot of the Ned Kelly gang whose personal act of treachery leads to their bloody deaths. At the opposite iconographic extreme is Patrick White's Mordecai Himmelfarb (*Riders in the Chariot*, 1961), this time the Jewish noble savage which can be regarded as an inversion of the more usual demonic Jew, now held up as the supreme paragon, the Jew who is so good as to be thoroughly boring – or at least thoroughly improbable and unknowable, perhaps the Australian answer to Forster's Professor Godbole. Just as there is an argument for proper linguistic recognition of gender difference and for racial and ethnic tolerance in multicultural Australia, so too there is an equal argument for the recognition of the anti-Jewish slur. I am talking about an awareness, not censorship, since it is all too easy to fall into the contemporary opposite trap of intolerant political correctness. While we might deplore the (postmodernist) taste of an author who, as it had been claimed, seems to want to glamorise brutality using 'literature' as the convenient excuse (a mainstay of popular cinema for so very long), there is also the question of free speech to be recognised, as well as the oddities of individual taste and idiosyncrasy which never cease to surprise. And there is also the argument that the notoriety this novel has received should at least serve to air some of the normally unspoken problems surrounding the business of evaluating literary works – something of special importance in relation to the granting of literary awards – that is, if people can really learn.

So things appear to go on much as before. Postmodernist amorality is intrinsic, relativist thinking which, curiously, is now widely, at least in theory, within our universities though not to the same degree in actual practice in the wider Australian community. One reason for the recent furore over *The Hand that Signed the Paper*, I suspect, is that this novel suddenly drew attention to the contradiction which had generally passed unnoticed. It brought into focus the fine balance between our acceptance of (communal, ethnic, minority) difference and our need to decide where the limits of relativism lie, where the line in the sand is ultimately to be drawn. Another reason has to do with the equally sensitive balance, this time in literature, between imaginative freedom and ethical constraint, a crucial issue which has yet to be fully explored and understood by theorists and literary commentators. In the meantime, so unaware, it seems, is the average or even the experienced Australian reader of the anti-Jewish stereotype, or else so deeply rooted in the reader's mind is the discursive representation of the Jew as a mere literary or poetic convention that, even on the rare occasion when such an instance is for once recognised or given attention, the whole matter tends to be regarded as quire harmless – which one would like to think it is. Jewish history, however, suggests otherwise.

Notes

1. Joshua Trachtenberg. *The Devil and the Jews: The Medieval Conception of the Jew and its Relation to Modern Anti-Semitism.* Jewish Publication Society of America, Philadelphia. 1943. Quoted from back cover.
2. Quoted from *Australian Book Review.* August 1995. 173. 19.
3. *Australian Book Review.* 17.
4. Nancy Keesing. John Lang and '*The Forger's Wife*'. John Ferguson, Sydney. 1979.
5. James Tucker, *Ralph Rashleigh.* Angus and Roberston, 1975. 77.
6. Alexander Harris. *The Emigrant Family or The Story of an Australian Settler,* ANU Press, Canberra, 1967, (1849) 99.
6. Quoted in Michael Blakeney. *Australia and the Jewish Refugees, 1933 – 1948.* Croom Helm, Australia. 1985.
8. Contained in *Marcus Clarke*
9. Julian Croft. *The Life and Opinions of Tom Collins: A Study of the Worlds of Joseph Furphy.* UQP, 1991. 228.
10. Quoted in *Australia and the Jewish Refugees 1933 – 1948.* 17.
11. *Jonah,* Endeavour Press, Aust. 1933 (1911). 12.
12. *Jonah,* 12.
13. *Jonah,* 164.
14. Hilary Rubinstein. *Chosen: The Jews in Australia.* Allen and Unwin. 1987. 73.
15. Dorothy Green. 'Louis Stone's *Jonah*: A Cinematic Novel' republished in *The Australian Nationalists* (ed. Chris Wallace-Crabbe), OUP, Melbourne, 1971. 174.
16. J.H.M. Abbott. *Castle Vane: A Romance of Bushranging on the Upper Hunter in the Olden Days.* Angus and Robertson, Sydney, 1920. 109.
17. Jean-Paul Sartre. *Portrait of an anti-Semite* (tr. Erik de Mauny), London. 1948. 40.
18. Charles Francis Adam de Brune. *Shadow Crook.* Angus and Robertson, Sydney, 1930.

19. In Julian Croft's 'Response to Modernism, 1915 – 1965'. *The* Penguin *New Literary History of Australia* (ed. Laurie Hergenhan), 1988, 417.
20. *The* Penguin *New Literary History of Australia.* 410.
21. *Chosen: The Jews in Australia.* 29.
22. Leon Gettler. *An Unpromised Land.* Fremantle Arts Centre Press. 1993. 41.
23. *An Unpromised Land.* 43.
24. *An Unpromised Land.* 94.
25. *Australia and the Jewish Refugees 1933 – 1948.* 186 – 187.
26. Contained in *Pomegranates: A Century of Jewish Australian Writing.* (ed. Gael Hammer), Millennium, 1988.
27. Based on John Thompson. *Five to Remember.* Lansdowne. 1964.
28. Artie Shaw. *The Trouble with Cinderella: An Outline of Identity.* DaCapo. 1979. 16.
29. Anne Sheppard, *Aesthetics: An Introduction to the Philosophy of Art,* OUP. 1987. 153.

PAST WRITINGS

CRNLE generated an enormous amount of writing either through its Review Journals or through its occasional collections dedicated to particular writers or particular themes. The selections below give an insight into the work that was produced.

'Freedom Became My Dancing Shoe': Liberty and the Pursuit of Happiness in the Work of Kamala Das

DOROTHY JONES

Kamala Das has written extensively of love – its pains, its disillusionments, and, much more rarely, its joys and delights. The frankness with which describes sexual passion has caused some uneasiness among readers in her native India and brought her a fair measure of notoriety, as her poem 'Loud Posters' suggests:

> I've stretched my two dimensional
> Nudity on sheets of weeklies, monthlies,
> Quarterlies, a sad sacrifice (SC, p. 29)

The air of sensationalism generated by such outspokenness in an Indian woman can easily distract readers from coming to terms with what Das's poetry and fiction actually have to say about sexuality in a society which expects women to be modest, submissive and unobtrusive is in itself an act of rebellion which imparts energy and vigour to much of Kamala Das's writing. But defiance is not in the end sufficient to break through the terrible constraints imposed by social custom and sexual convention. Das's principal achievement has been to define and expose the prison in which a woman finds herself trapped, rather than proclaiming an escape route out of it, although she also records the urge to escape and a desperate longing for freedom.

A characteristic feature of her poems is their coolly cynical view of male/female relationships. 'The Looking Glass' (D, p. 25) is a trenchant example. Lines 1–16 ('Getting a man to love you ... Endless female hungers') provide an interesting variation on Virginia Woolf's comment: 'Women have served all these centuries as looking-glasses possessing the magic and delicious power of reflecting the figure of a man at twice its natural size'.[1] But the conclusion of Das's poem modulates from cynicism into bitter lament. However vain and egotistical the lover, his departure leaves the speaker's life bleak, empty and meaningless: 'now drab and destitute'. Cool observation of male limitations offers little protection against love's desolation.

Although the woman's dilemma is often portrayed in very personal terms, there is also awareness of the pressures imposed by social attitudes and institutions. Many of Das's poems present the image of a marriage which had grown lifeless and unsatisfying. 'The Joss-sticks at Cadell Road' opens with an evocative account of the corpses of the poor being carried to funeral pyres behind Cadell Road in Bombay. Dark-skinned and gaunt, garlanded with flowers and 'scented up/To smell like a low-paid Street girl', the bodies resemble joss-sticks thrust into the flame to ascend as incense to heaven. Death is related to sexuality through the image of the street girl which in turn contrast with the reference to the crones who follow the procession,

> Wailing flatly and
> Monotonously
> As only the poor
> And the absolutely
> Hopeless know how to wail. (D, p. 23)

The burning of the corpse is described in an image of animal ferocity – 'the fire/Leapt high, snarling, beast-like' – and the animal image is continued in the reference to a 'queue' of seagulls', those scavenger birds who ride the waves where the garlands formerly binding the corpse have been thrown. The poem ends with an apparent change of subject.

> My husband said, I think I shall
> Have a beer, it's hot,
> Very hot today.
> And I thought, I must
> Drive fast to town and
> Lie near my friend for an hour. I
> Badly need some rest.

Like the funeral, the marriage is an image of death, but, lacking the funeral's association with colour, intensity and deep feeling, the marriage is seen as stable, empty and dull. In her autobiography *My Story* Kamala Das describes her own marriage as unsatisfying and unfulfilling. It is a little hard to know how to respond to this book which, while adopting an openly confessional tone, conceals quite as much or more as it reveals. But if considered as a literary rather than a factual recreation of a writer's life, it often serves as an illuminating comment on her poetry and fiction, exploring many of the same dilemmas and situations. She writes of her husband:

> He was obsessed with sex. If it was not for sex, it was the Co-operative Movement in India, and both of these bored me. But I endured both, knowing that there was no escape from either. I even learnt to pretend an interest that I never once really felt.
>
> As my boss says, said my husband one day, the Co-operative Movement has failed, but eh Co-operative Movement must succeed. I thought that I would burst out laughing. Who is your boss, I asked him. It is Ventkatappiah, formerly of the ICS. Have you not heard of him?
>
> My husband was furious. He felt I was not up-to-date with the happenings in the field if co-operation. You have not once touched the prestigious report of Rural Credit Survey

> Committee, he said. But I let you make love to me every night
> I said, isn't that good enough? (p. 135)

In 'Composition' the speaker claims that her husband offered her freedom – 'as much as you want' – but in doing so place under intense pressure.

> Freedom became my dancing shoe,
> How well I danced,
> and danced without rest,
> until the shoes turned grimy on my feet
> and I began to have doubts, (D, p. 30)

Other poems, however, associate marriage with constraint rather than freedom. In 'The Sunshine Car' the husband locks his wife in 'a room of books' (SC, p. 49), and although the poem 'I shall Some Day',

> the cocoon,
> You built around me with morning tea,
> Love-words flung from doorways of course
> Your tires lust (SC, p. 49)

is not specifically identified with marriage, it does seem to represent the constant and continuing relationship from which the woman threatens to take flight into freedom not unlike that afforded by the grimy dancing shoe, only to return one day seeking shelter 'here in your nest of familiar scorn'. Even though in another poem the husband is compared to a spider, he is not portrayed as cruel, merely uncomprehending and indifferent to his wife's emotional needs, making flight impossible by transforming her into stone:

> Fond husband, ancient settler in the mind,
> Old fat spider, weaving webs of bewilderment,

> Be kind. You turn me into a bird of stone, a granite
> Dove, you build round me a shabby drawing room,
> And stroke my pitted face absent-mindedly while
> You read. ('The Stone Age', Op, p. 51)

Instead of displaying the soft gentleness of the dove, the wife has hardened into granite, and the stone bird is yet another image of emotional deadness within marriage.

Although love affairs offer one possible escape from the prison of an unhappy marriage, these also entrap the woman, either because the lover departs, leaving behind a terrible sense of loss and longing, or else, depressingly, he comes to resemble a second husband. Throughout the poetry images of constraint and confinement are associated even more powerfully and more frequently with extra-marital relationships than with marriage.

> I enter others'
> Lives, and
> Make of every trap of lust
> A temporary home. ('Glass', OP, p. 21)

'The Bangles' describes a relationship from which passion is ebbing.

> At night
> In sleep, the woman lashes
> At pillows with bangled arms; in
> Vain, she begs bad dreams to fade. (SC, pp. 34–5)

The bangles resemble manacles and are associated earlier in the poem with the flower garlands adorning a corpse. In 'Captive' the speaker expresses relief at breaking free from her most recent lover, 'so long so long sweet/slavery' but she is forced to recognise that the labyrinthine spider web in which remains trapped is of her own choosing:

> For years I have run from one
> Gossamer lane to another, I am
> Now my own captive. (D, p. 17)

For a woman who lies buried beneath a man's six-foot frame, the whole world narrows to the dimensions of his body ('The Conflagration', D, p. 20), and in 'The Prisoner' she is compared to a convict seeking to comprehend the ground-plan of the prison in search of an exit as she studies her lover's body hoping to find 'An escape from its snare' (OP, p. 29). The immobilising anguish of such a relationship is a kind of crucifixion.

> We have lain in every weather, nailed, not, not
> To crosses, but to soft beds ... ('The Descendants', D, p. 8)

Another image which Kamala Das repeatedly associates with the dissatisfactions, disappointments and constraints of love is theatrical performance. Sometimes the images of theatre and prison coalesce.

> Life lay huddled in prisoner's robes
> Waiting for an easy extinction.
> I sat in a gallery seat and looked
> Till my insomniac eyes ached
> But that was how I grew. ('Afterwards', SC, p. 57)

In 'Drama' the poet envisages herself as a tragedienne playing, 'Black gowned, black veiled', in a tiny theatre to an audience who receives with derision her wailings, breast-beatings and talk of unrequited love. Similarly, when she is with her lover, she plays her role knowing that he responds with inward mirth (SC, p. 62). Acting a part is restrictive, since actors must accept direction and speak the lines they are given – 'I am the puppet on this string' ('The Swamp', OP, p. 53). Imagery of theatrical performance underlines both the need to maintain an appearance of social conformity by playing the role of the happily married woman, and the ephemerality of love's drama. Ironically, the role of passionate mistress may be as much a pose that of 'happy woman/Happy wife'.

> It's only
> To save my face, I flaunt at
> Times a grand, flamboyant lust.
> ('The Freaks', SC, p. 10)

If, in assuming the role mistress, the woman takes her part in a play, she may find that her lover is also performing a part that can subsequently be filled by a number of actors. In 'The Substitute', the speaker performs both as wife and mistress. She compares herself to a coastline against which the sea of memory continually breaks, with each wave bringing a further recollection of the lost and longed-for lover, while in a grotesque charade she goes through the motions of role as married woman.

> It will all right when I learn
> To paint my mouth like clown's
> It will be all right if I put my hair,
> Stand near my husband to make a proud pair. (D, p. 6)

There is much in the poem to suggest it is ideal of love which had eluded her, far more than the actual lover: … 'I only lost/ Lost all, lost even/What I never had'. Although she continues to seek this ideal, the hollowness of her marriage is echoed in the hollowness of her various love affairs.

> After that love became a swivel-door
> When one went out another came in
> Then I lost count, for always in my arms
> Was a substitute for a substitute. (D, p. 7)

The motifs of theatre, prison, husband and lover come together in one Das's finest poems 'The Old Playhouse'. As in 'The Stone Age' the woman is compared to a bird, this time a swallow which files vast distances to live continually in the summer season. Now it is the lover, not the husband, who seeks to hold the bird captive by creating around her a perpetual summer season so that she will forget her very nature and the urge to fly which is so central to it. The fact that summer in India can be a very oppressive season is central to poem's meaning.

> Your room is
> Always lit by artificial lights, your windows always Shut.
> Even the air-conditioner helps so little,
> All pervasive is the male scent of your breath. The cut flowers
> In the vases have begun to smell human sweat. (OP, p. 1)

The woman is not only restricted and diminished by her lover's attentions, she loses her will, her capacity for reason and her joy in living.

> There is
> No more singing, no more dance, my mind is an old
> Playhouse with all its lights put out. (OP, p. 1)

Instead of performing on stage, she herself is transformed into the darkened theatre where, it is implied no further performance will ever take place. To fly is both to escape and to soar above the earth, so it is significant that the trapped bird should symbolise the situation both of wife ('The Stone Age') and of mistress ('The Old Playhouse), for this lover had become merely another husband who expects his mistress to act out the role of wife, proffering sweetness and nourishment.

> You called me wife,
> I was taught to break saccharine into your tea and
> To offer at the right moment the vitamins.

The metamorphosis of lover into husband is explore from a different point of view in Kamala Das's short story 'Sanatan Choudhuri's Wife'. Gopi Menon, becoming suspicious when his sleeping wife murmurs the name 'Sanatan', secretly follows her early one morning, after he is supposed to have left for work, to see her enter a luxurious house and spies her through the window having breakfast with the owner. When he rings the doorbell, both the servants and their master, Sanatan Choudhuri, are so matter of fact in their references to the Mem Saheb that Menon becomes totally confused over the distinction between reality and illusion. Despite the evidence of his own eyes, he accepts that the woman in the house is Sanatan Choudhuri's wife, not his.

> Menon could not bring himself to give a backward glance at the lady wearing blue although she resembled his wife to a remarkable degree. Suspicion is a kind of poison-weed he told himself as he walked to the nearest bus-stop. (DCP, p. 81)

While the woman shares a life of wealth and privilege with her lover, she is unable, even with him, to escape the role of wife and all the limitations it entails.

Yet many of the poems express a deep hunger for love. However inadequate the lovers described in them prove to be, they have been conjured up by the woman's need of them.

> It was my desire that made him male
> And beautiful, so that when at last we
> Met, to believe that once I knew not his
> Form, his quiet touch, or the blind kindness
> Of his lips was hard indeed. ('A Relationship', SC, p. 18)

Through love, the woman in 'The Old Playhouse' hopes to grow in self-knowledge and extend the boundaries of her life, only to be disappointed once again.

> It was not to gather knowledge
> Of yet another man that I came to you but to learn
> What I was, and by learning, to learn to grow, but every
> Lesson you gave was about yourself. (OP, p. 1)

But although love, with all its grief and betrayal, closes in like a trap, it is still represented as something to be sought after. Kamala Das's poetry chronicles a female quest for transcendence – an attempt to move beyond the limits of self. Both the quest and its failure are represented from time to time in her work through reference to an episode in Hindu mythology, the love between Radha and the god Krishna, which she uses to indicate the two extremes love has to offer, ecstatic abandon on the one hand, and on the other, a sense of devastating loss leasing to a death-in-life existence.

For centuries the legend of how Krishna, eighth avatar of Vishnu, spent his child hood and youth among cowherds and their wives as Brindaban on the banks of the rive Jumna has inspired Indian writers and artists. All the cowherds' wives, the gopis, fell passionately in love with Krishna, and although one, Radha, was singled out as particularly dear to him, he multiplied himself many times so he could dance and make love with all the gopis simultaneously. Details of the story are presented very erotically in painting, literature and devotional writing, and there have been comparisons drawn between the frank sexuality of this tradition of Indian mysticism and the mystical writing of St John of the Cross and St Theresa of Avila.[2] The Krishna legend, particularly in its account of the god's relationship with the gopis, had become an important focus in Hinduism for Bhakti, the experience of intense religious adoration in which the soul abandons itself in ecstasy to the divine.

> God is in love with the soul, and the soul with god. In this divine love-affair God is necessarily the male, the soul the female: God takes the initiative and the soul must passively wait for the divine embrace.[3]

Radha becomes a prototype of the human soul and the rasa-lila, the spring-time dance during which all the gopis were sexually united with the multiple Krishna, is not a historical reality, but an eternal event located in the human heart.[4]

In art, the legend is often presented with an ambivalence similar to that surrounding the cult of courtly love in medieval European literature where the boundaries between the carnal and the spiritual are frequently left uncertain. The detailed descriptions of sexual union between Krishna and Radha in Indian devotional literature are presented 'unequivocally necessary to the super-structure of endless, transcendent Desire, the inner fire of Bhakti'.[5] Kamala Das is fully aware of this ambivalence when she uses Radha's love for Krishna as an image of the transcendent bliss and union with the divine which a woman may experience through sexual love.

> The long waiting
> Had made their bond so chaste, and all the doubting
>
> And the reasoning
> So that in his first true embrace, she was girl
> And virgin crying
> Everything in me
> Is melting, even the hardness at the core
> O Krishna, I am melting, melting, melting
>
> Nothing remains but
> You ... ('Rhada', D, p. 9)

In her autobiography Das associates her own devotion to Krishna with her feelings about the various men in her life. She describes how, on her wedding night, ignorant and frightened by her husband's sexual advances, she urged, much to his astonishment, that they both pray to Krishna first. She also describes how, in her initial disappointment with both marriage and husband, she was certain she would have a son who resembled Krishna.

> Through the smoke of the incense I saw the beauteous smile of my Krishna. Always, always, I shall love you I told him, not speaking aloud but willing Him to hear me, only you will be my husband, only your horoscope will match with mine, (MS, p. 96)

The language leaves it unclear whether her prayer was addressed to the god or her unborn child. Later in *My Story* Das associates her search for love with longing for the god. Describing her association with a man who failed to live up to her expectations she writes

> I was perhaps seeking a familiar face that blossomed like a blue lotos in the waters of my dreams. It was to get closer to that bodyless one that I approached other forms and lost my way. (MS, p. 124)

Later she comments:

> I was looking for an ideal lover. I was looking for the one who went to Matthura and forgot to return to his Radha ... Subconsciously I hoped for the death of my ego. I was looking for an executioner whose axe would cleave my head in two. (MS, p. 180)

Although the love of Radha and Krishna serves as a ready symbol for the ecstatic union between lovers and for the soul's desire to merge with the godhead, it can easily be associated with experiences of loss and longing, since Radha was temporarily estranged from Krishna through her jealousy over his love for the other gopis. Eventually the god abandoned all the other gopis, leaving them distraught and desolate, when he gave up his pastoral life at Brindiban to continue his career on earth as a great prince at Mathura. In this period of his life he married his principal consort Rukmini, and over sixteen thousand other wives besides. Although still a fervent lover, his love now becomes 'sanctioned and formalised by legal marriage'.[6] For all its mystical significance, Krishna's relationship with

Radha and the other gopis was adulterous. There are legends that when Radha's husband, Ayanagosha, sought to surprise the lovers, Krishna transformed himself into a goddess (Kali in one version, Durga in another) so that Radha appeared to be engaged in an innocent act of devotion in which her husband joined.[7] But the breaking of social ties through adultery could also signify the soul's readiness to abandon all social considerations for the sake of the god.

> By worldly standards, they [Radha and the gopis] were committing the gravest of offences but they were doing it for Krishna who was God himself. They were setting God above home and duty, they were leaving everything for love of God and in surrendering their honour were providing the most potent symbol of what devotion meant.[8]

Das shows herself aware of the ironies implicit in her use of legend. Even as a child she had noted its adulterous implications when she assumed her female relatives' fear and distaste for the subject of sexuality was inspired by the many stories of sexual violence in Hindu mythology.

> The only one heroine whose sex life seemed comparatively untumultuous was Radha who waited on the banks of the Jumna for her blueskinned lover. But she was another's wife and so an adulteress. In the orbit of elicit sex there seemed to be only crudeness and violence. (MS, p. 26)

The human lovers Das portrays in her poetry may inspire the same passionate devotion as Krishna, but usually they depart, just as he did, proving themselves in the meantime to be fallible and most ungodlike. In her poem 'The Maggots' she again use the Krishna legend, this time to express the suffering and disappointments of love together with the emptiness of the marriage relationship.

> At sunset, on the river bank, Krishna
> Loved her for the last time and left ...

> That night in her husband's arms, Radha felt
> So dead that he asked, what is wrong,
> Do you mind my kisses, love? and she said,
> No, not at all, but thought, What is
> It to the corpse if the maggots nip? (D, p. 22)

Love of Krishna is one way of expressing a woman's quest for self-transcendence and freedom from social obligations, but Das also links the Krishna theme to images of imprisonment and entrapment. In My Story she describes her relationship with a dark-skinned man reputed to be a great libertine whom she identifies quite specifically with Krishna.

> You are my Krishna, I whispered kissing his eyes shut. He laughed. I felt that I was a virgin in his arms. Was there a summer before the autumn of his love? Was there a dawn before the dusk of his skin? I do not remember. I carried him with me inside my eyelids, the dark God of girlhood dreams. At night from the lush foxholes of the city his concubines wailed for him. Oh Krishna, oh Kanhaiya, do not leave me for another. (MS, pp. 190–191)

Details of this relationship, and even some of the phrases used to describe it in *My Story*, also recur in a short story 'The Sign of the Lion' and in several poems. Particular reference is made to a room in a man's house which contained eighteen mirrors.

> There were eighteen mirrors in his room, eighteen ponds into which I dipped my hot brown body. (MS, p. 191)

In 'The Sign of the Lion' the female narrator describes the room where she embraces the dark-skinned lover who reminds her of Krishna as having mirrors on three sides: 'The mirrors inhibit my lovemaking, I feel that I am taking part in a group orgy' (DCP, p. 74). Mirrors reflecting lovers are also subject of a poem, 'The Motif in the Mirror'.

Outside the rain had ceased. We closed the
 verandah door. All the blue
Lights were on. How shall I describe that first
 embrace – you have not seen
The many mirrors in his room. When we embraced,
 we fell in their
Cerulean pools as a deathless motif, repeating,
 repeating,
And repeating, this reflection of a reflection,
 this shadow of
A shadow, this dream of a dream, and I knew him
 then by knowing who
I was, and knew my self by knowing who he was
 but he said,
Rising from my side, it is eight, get up sweet
 wife, I'll take you home.[9]

The association of the multiple reflections in the mirrors with the image of swimming is important. Among the scenes from Krishna's life most profusely illustrated in Indian art are his stealing the gopis clothes as they swim in the Jumna, the god sporting with the gopis in the water and the rasa-lila where Krishna multiplies himself so he can make love with all the gopis simultaneously. Kamala Das almost certainly has such mythic episodes in mind when she describes the lovers surrounded by their myriad reflections. In her poem, 'The Suicide', swimming is an image of freedom, initially the freedom of innocence, then freedom obtained through sexual indulgence, and finally a freedom gained through abandoning the world of material existence. 'The Motif in the Mirror' combines images of reflection and plunging into water to convey a sense of release through ecstatic union, where the lovers in knowing one another each come to know themselves. But the mirror tends to be a very negative image in Das's writing because it is usually associated with limitation. In her poem 'The Looking Glass' and again in 'Gino' the woman, through her reflection in the mirror, presents herself as an object of her lover's delectation, a situation reinforced in 'Gino' by the fact that the man is European not Indian.

> I shall serve myself in
> Bedroom-mirrors, dark fruit on silver platter,
> While he lies watching, fair conqueror of another's
> Country. (OP, p. 13)

The poem 'With its Quiet Tongue' represents the speaker's heart as a pale green mirror gazed on by a succession of men who see only themselves. Here the mirror is a dead end because its hard cold surface merely reflects those who look into it without being able to relate to them.

> They looked in with timid eyed, hungry
> Perhaps for flattery, and smiled
> Their happiest smile before they
> Walked away ...
>
> They left the mirror cold, and so
> Beautiful; how much kinder to have
> Left a great, sprawling crack shaped
> Like a spider's web ... (SC, p. 32)

So, although the multiple reflections in 'The Motif in the Mirror' symbolise the fulfilment and transcendence attainable through sexual union, the anti-climactic ending when the lover, addressing the woman as 'wife', rouses her to take her back to her own home, and, presumably, he own husband makes clear the illusory nature of such visionary joys. Mirrors reveal only bodies, and in poem after poem Kamala Das emphasises that bodies are prisons and lovers one another's captives, with the woman more closely constrained than the man. In her autobiography she writes of the man with the many-mirrored bedroom: 'His body became my prison, I could not see beyond it' (MS, p. 193). Her poem 'The Old Playhouse', describing how imprisoned a woman feels by her lover's presence, also ends with the image, drawn from classical Greek mythology, in which mirror and water coalesce.

> For, love is Narcissus at the water's edge, haunted
> By its own lovely face and yet it must seek at last
> An end, a pure, total freedom, it must will the mirrors
> To shatter and the kind night to erase the water (OP, pp. 1–2)

Instead of self-knowledge she hoped for, the relationship provides the woman with a reflection of her loneliness and isolation. Now the mirror becomes a prison because it represents the confining boundaries of the self which the speaker must somehow gather the will to break through, even at the risk of death itself.

Kamala Das's poetry presents in very individual and personal terms the situation of a woman trapped within a loveless relationship from which she seeks release through romantic passion only to find this equally unsatisfying and restrictive. But there are also a number of indications that such a situation is not merely personal but imposed on women by society. In her novella 'A Doll for the Child Prostitute', Das explores at some length the sexual pressures society places on women to force them into a trap from which death seems the only way out.

> My first school-house
> is now a brothel
> and
> the ladies sun themselves on the lawn
> in the afternoons
> with their greying hair
> newly washed,
> left undyed.

> Who can say, looking at them,
> that they are toys
> fit for the roaring nights? (D, p. 33)

These lines from 'Composition' form an appropriate comment on the plight of Rukmani, central character of the novella, who in one day is transformed from schoolgirl into whore, and while still enough to play with toys herself becomes a plaything for men old enough to be her grandfather.

> It was the same old story. The stepfather raping the minor girl while her mother was out visiting her relatives. The fat woman called Ayee by the inmates of the house threw back her head and laughed aloud. 'Anasuya, what did you expect from a bum like your Govind', she asked the thin visitor who had brought her twelve year old daughter for sale.
>
> (DCP, p. 9)

Rukmani quickly makes friends with the fourteen year old Sita who has been sold to Ayee by a village procurer at the age of ten after the rest of her family died of cholera. Sex means a very little to the two girls who are preoccupied with dolls and games of hopscotch from which they have to be dragged to attend to clients.

> For them it came as an occasional punishment meted out for some obscure reason. Perhaps the mistake they committed was they were born as girls in a society that regarded the female as a burden, a liability. (DCP, p. 36)

The world of the brothel is a paradigm of the women's lives in a society at large determined, dictated and limited by their sexuality. At the other end of the scale from the two little girls is the old hag Sindhuthai who once ran a brothel herself.

> My favourite girl threw me out calling me names. What could I do? I was past the age for attracting any man. All I could do was roam around looking for a hut to live in, a shelter over my head. I begged at street corners for a year. Then I became a useful member of this locality. I could perform abortions for

> as little as twenty rupees. So you invited me into your houses. I was lucky. (DCP, p. 31)

The horror and pathos of the situation is merely one strand woven into the complex and various pattern of life created within the story. Ayee and Rukmani's mother are stupid rather than evil, and even Inspector Saheb, the corrupt policeman who represents the oppressive world of male authority which bears down upon the inmates of the brothel, is also a sad figure with his mouldy smelling scalp 'where white hair grew in untidy patches'. There is savage irony in the way the two little girls' services are appropriated by substantial family men. Sita's regular patron is a school teacher with three grown up daughters in College, and the Inspector Saheb is attracted to Rukmani because she reminds him of his grand-daughter. But despite this, the world of the story is one in which people with limited social expectations, living under the heavy burdens imposed by poverty, shift for themselves as best they can.

As in her poetry, Kamala Das uses mythological reference in A Doll for the Child Prostitute to draw attention to the female predicament. By naming the two children after great queens of legend, Das further emphasises their vulnerability. Rukmini was Krishna's queen and Sita, heroine of the Indian epic the Ramayana, was married to Rama, seventh avatar of Vishnu. Ayee the calculating and prosperous madam, who tries to mould the girls in her own image, is appropriately named after the goddess of fortune and giver of wealth, Lachmi. As Vishnu's wife, Lachmi was reborn as his consort in each of his reincarnations.

> When he became Rama she was the faithful Sita, born of a furrow in a ploughed field. When he was incarnated as Krishna, she entered both phases of his life: as the cowgirl Radha and as his wife Rukmini. [10]

Although one of the adult prostitutes is named Radha, the

young man called Krishna, who is a regular client, directs his attentions not to her, but to the elegant and beautiful Mira. Through ironic implication Ayee's brothel is mockingly compared to the idyllic Brindaban. Krishna and Mira sing and read together from the Gita Govinda, a twentieth century Sanskrit poem in which the love of Radha and Krishna is described the erotic language and imagery reminiscent of the Song of Songs. But, as is often the case in Das's writing, the Krishna figure proves disappointingly human. When Ayee discovers he spends his time talking politics, rather than making love, she asks if he is impotent, and then goes on to admonish him: 'This is a brothel ... not a conference hall' (DCP, p. 19). Arrested by the Inspector Saheb after marrying and eloping with Mira, he turns out to be only nineteen, without a job, and childishly relieved when Ayee insists he return to his mother, leaving the unhappy Mira back in the brothel, dispossessed now of her position as favourite and the room of her own which went with it.

The brothel and all it represents defeats any hopes, capacities or aspirations which might lead a woman to express or fulfil herself outside the narrowly determined confines imposed on her as a sexual being. Rukmani is in the sixth standard, able to read Marathi and Hindi and beginning to learn English. But when, on her arrival in the brothel, she drops her satchel of books on the sleeping mat she shares with Sita, it is clear that her education and any further possibility of intellectual development have come to a full stop. Mira, the 'matriculate', seeks her fulfilment through poetry and romantic love. She identifies herself with the fifteenth century princess, Mira Bai, who wrote poetry in praise of Krishna and began a widespread popular movement[11]: 'It is not strange that I am Mira and he is Krishna?' Like the princess poet, the prostitute Mira seeks to dedicate her life to her young Krishna, discarding profligacy for marriage – a decision which others in the brothel consider immoral and scandalous. But romantic love proves a disappointment and a snare, and Mira ends much worse than she began. As Ayee explains to Rukmani:

> Failing in love with men is a dangerous thing ... It is like tying oneself with a rope. If you do not love any man you remain free. (DCP, p. 52)

The girl most likely to succeed in life is Saraswati, named after the goddess of learning and wisdom.

> Saraswati was the most qualified of the lot, the one was totally devoid of emotion and was the most professional of all. (DCP, p. 55)

She already has money at her disposal and will one day end as Madam of her own house. But her success involves the denial of emotion and the acceptance of the sexual role society has forced upon her. She can prosper, and even attain a measure of independence, but only as a whore.

Rukmani's friend Sita alone succeeds in escaping the life of the brothel, but for her the way out is death. When the onset of puberty coincides with pregnancy, Ayee summons Sinduthai to abort her, and a fatal haemorrhage results. In Rukmani's eyes the dying Sita resembles the expensive European doll Inspector Saheb has promised to but her.

> Ayee and Radha were tucking old sarees between Sita's thighs. Blood was soaking through the clothes rapidly. Sita lay insensate like a doll. How pale she looked with the rash of the midday sun mottling her narrow face. She resembled a foreign doll. Only her belly seemed alive, protruding from her flat body like a growth. Would she utter Mummy when she was pressed on her tummy, like that expensive doll? (DCP, p. 44)

Alive, Sita had been a toy for men who patronised the brothel, and now, in evidence of her total powerlessness, her dead body resembles one of the dolls she used to play with. The poignancy of a situation where death is the only escape from the trap of sexuality is also echoed in Das's poetry. Age delivers a woman from the more immediate sexual pressures, but it renders her pathetic and ridiculous, leading eventually into the darkness of death.

> ... I shall be the grandmother
> Willing away her belongings, those scraps and trinkets
> More lasting than her bones. Perhaps some womb in that
> Darker world shall convulse, when I finally enter,
> A legitimate entrant marked by discontent.
> ('Gino', OP, p. 14)

The convulsion in the womb, with its associations of sexuality and birth, suggests that in death alone will not release an individual from the cycle of existence.

> Even
> oft-repeated moves
> of every scattered cell
> will give no power
> to escape
> from cages on involvement.
> I must linger on,
> trapped in immortality,
> my only freedom to
> decompose. (D, p. 35)

Death is merely a stepping-stone to another life, and only if the soul succeeds in blending with the godhead can it achieve deliverance from the never-ending cycle of death and rebirth.[12] But in her poem 'The Suicide' Das, through images of swimming and drowning, hints at the possibility of liberation. The speaker contemplates drowning herself so that the sea will divide her soul from her body. Love has eluded her and she longs for death: 'If love is not to be had, I want to be dead'. Ironically, however, swimming is one thing she does really well – 'It comes naturally to me'. As a child she swam in the pale green pond alongside her Malabar house.

> I swam about and floated,
> I lay speckled green and gold
> In all the hours of the sun.

Her grandmother's warning that she is now too big to swim naked in the pond, puts an end to his freedom which, as an adult, she tries to recover in her lover's arms.

> The white man who offers
> Himself as a stiff drink,
> Is for me,
> To tell the truth,
> Only water.
> Only a pale-green pond
> Glimmering in the sun.
> In him I swim
> All broken with longing.

'Only water' counteracts the sly phallic imagery of 'a stiff drink', while 'broken with longing' adds a harsher note the simple enjoyment associated earlier in the poem with swimming in the pale green pond. Love, like water, is impossible to hold onto. The illusory freedom afforded by swimming is paralleled by images of drowning which releases the soul to enter the vortex of the sea.

> The sea's inner chambers
> Are all very warm.
> There must be a sun slumbering
> At the vortex of the sea.

> The poem concludes with the lines,
> Only the soul knows how to sing
> At the vortex of the sea.

The singing soul may represent not only joy, but creative energy. In an earlier poem 'The Wild Bougainvillea' Das presents a woman who frees herself from longing for a lost lover through her absorption in the sights and sounds of the city she lives in. Although many of these are ugly and sombre, they are also associated with flowering and growth.

> But, I did see beside
> The older tombs some marigolds bloom and the
> Wild red bougainvillea
> Climbing the minaret. I walked, I saw and
> I heard, the city tamed
> Itself for me, and then my hunger for a
> Particular touch waned
> And one day I sent him some roses and slept
> Through the night, a silent
> Dreamless sleep and woke up in the morning free.
> (SC, p. 17)

There are one or two other poems which suggest that the creative imagination is a source of freedom and power, but the overwhelming image which comes through Kamala Das's writing as a whole is of a woman trapped by the nature of her sexuality and the social limitations imposed on her because of it. She may possibly attain freedom, but it is likely to be at the cost of life itself.

Notes

1. Virginia Woolf, *A Room of One's Own* (Harmondsworth: Penguin Books, 1974), p. 37.
2. R.C. Zaehner, *Hinduism* (Oxford: Oxford University Press, 1966), p. 129.
3. *Ibid.*, p. 127.
4. M.S. Randhawa, *The Krishna Legend in Pahari Painting* (New Delhi: Lalit Kala Akademi, 1956) no page numbers.
5. Philip Rawson, *The Art of Tantra* (London: Thames and Hudson, 1973), p. 100.
6. W.G. Archer, *The Loves of Krishna in Indian Painting and Poetry* (London: Allen and Unwin, 1957), p. 63.
7. See W.J. Wilkins, *Hindu Mythology, Vedic and Paranic* (London: Curzon Press, 1974, first published 1882), p. 210, and P. Thomas, *Epics Myths and Legends of Indian: A Comprehensive Survey of the Hindus, Buddhists and Jains* (Bombay: D.P. Taraporevala Sons &Co., 13th ed., 1973), p. 77.
8. Archer, p. 75.
9. This poem is not included in Kamala Das's books of verse, but is quoted by Devindra Kohli in *Kamala Das* (New Delhi: Arnold-Heinemann, 1975), pp. 115–116.
10. Veronica Ions, *Indian Mythology* (London: Paul Hamlyn, 1967), p. 91.
11. Archer, p. 84.
12. *Ibid.*, p. 17

The Two Sides of the Same Coin: Imaginative Fusion

V.S. Naipaul, *The Enigma of Arrival. A Novel in Five Sections*, Viking for Penguin Books, Ltd., 1987, £10.95.

YASMINE GOONERATNE
MACQUARIE UNIVERSITY

V.S. Naipaul's new novel shares its title with a surrealist painting by Giorgio de Chirico, a detail from which adorns its jacket. Let the novelist describe it:

> A classical scene, Mediterranean, ancient Roman – or so I saw it. A wharf; in the background, beyond walls and gateways there is the top of the mast of an antique vessel; on an otherwise deserted street in the foreground there are two figures, both muffled, one perhaps the person who has arrived, the other perhaps a native of the port. The scene is of desolation and mystery: it speaks of the mystery of arrival.

Naipaul goes on to describe a story that he fancied he might write some day about that scene in the Chirico painting.

> My story was to be set in classical times, in the Mediterranean. My narrator would arrive – for a reason I had yet to work out – at that classical port with the walls and gateways like cutouts. He would walk past that muffled figure on the quayside. He would move from that silence and desolation, that blankness, to a gateway or door. He would enter there and be swallowed by the life and noise of a crowded city. The mission he had come on would give him encounters and adventures. He would enter interiors, of houses and temples. Gradually there would come to him a feeling that he was getting nowhere; he would lose his sense of mission; he would begin to know only that he was lost. His feeling of adventure would give way to panic. He would want to escape, to get back to the quayside and his ship. But he wouldn't know how. I imagined some

> religious ritual in which, led on by kindly people, he would unwittingly take part and find himself the intended victim. At the moment of crisis he would come upon a door, open it, and find himself back on the quayside of arrival. He has been saved; the world is as he remembered it. Only one thing is missing now. Above the cut-out walls there is no mast, no sail. The antique ship has gone. The traveller has lived out his life.

This was the story, Naipaul adds, that oddly enough echoed the central theme of a book he was already writing at the time, and which we know under the title, *In A Free State*. It is also the focus, as the shared title indicates, of this new novel, in which a writer born in Trinidad lives for two years in a cottage in the grounds of a manor house in Wiltshire, recovering his health and creative energy after a series of debilitating experiences. Describing the changes which occur during that period in that place, and in the people among whom he lives, Naipaul's narrator describes also the nature of the writing life, the sources and process of a writer's inspiration and effort. Because the narrator is a writer, because he is an Indian from the West Indies who comes to Britain in the 1960s and achieves literary success and recognition there, it is easy to identify him with his creator who, as we all are aware, shares these experiences. It is important, I think, to be aware of that inclination as we read. For here, in this novel, Naipaul confronts the weaknesses and dissonances he and others have detected in his own career, and strives to heal a division that is not merely personal but implicit in the cultural dilemmas forced on every writer, Australian or West Indian, whose literary history has its roots in the experience of colonisation.

In an article on English painting of the 18th century, the West Indian poet and critic David Dabydeen noted a few years ago that the great English art collectors of the period were often men who had built their fortunes on sugar plantations in Trinidad and Jamaica. So that, as Dabydeen memorably put it, the estates hacked at by tortured and crippled black slaves and those other magnificently landscaped 'estates' in Wiltshire and Suffolk surrounding beautiful mansions in which works of art were hung, were two sides – literally – of the same coin. Dabydeen's article came back to me as I read *The Enigma of Arrival*, for in it Naipaul succeeds in bringing together imaginatively, through the artifice of fiction, the two sides of social and historical experience that had been materially linked but at the same time spiritually separated by the colonial experience.

V.S. Naipaul is today a famous name. The author of so many books, the winner of so many literary prizes, and the object of so much critical attention that many new readers might, like the erudite and otherwise very well-read bookseller I met the other day in Sydney, decide that it's too late to begin reading him now. Where is one to start? With the early satirical novels set in Trinidad? With the novel in which Naipaul showed himself able to write knowledgeably and sympathetically about British people living 'ordinary', British lives, *Mr Stone and the Knight's Companion?* With his novel set in Africa, *A Bend in the River?* With the controversial non-fiction in which Naipaul has made himself a reputation for devastating frankness (some might say insensitivity) and penetrating social analysis (some might say superficial observation): travel-books about India, South America, the West Indies, and the Islamic societies of West and Southeast Asia? Or with that early and brilliant novel, *A House For Mr Biswas,* which Naipaul published in 1960 to general, if rather astonished, acclaim? Britain's literary establishment speculated at the time as to the source of the enormous talent of this young, comparatively unknown author from the West Indies. How had he been able to immortalise in fiction a region which, together with Ireland, Dryden had consigned to ridicule in the 18th century as the eternal home of Dullness?

In *Mr Biswas* Naipaul gave a fictional rendering of the life of his late father, a Trinidad journalist. His hero triumphs, in his necessarily small and minor way, over the forces in his family, his society, and his own mind which might have kept him dependent on the charity and good humour of others. The novel was written as a memorial to the author's father, and as a celebration of that heroic life which set Naipaul (and incidentally, his younger brother Shiva to whose memory *Enigma of Arrival* is dedicated) free to develop as a writer and go his own way as his father had been unable to do. Both *Biswas* and *Enigma* contain biographical and autobiographical elements, but both are products, essentially, of the art of fiction. And the gaps that *Biswas* leaves in our knowledge of its writer, *Enigma* does much to fill in.

In the *New York Review of Books*, Naipaul wrote recently of his personal experience of a writer's life. 'The point that has always worried me,' he wrote,

> was one of vocabulary, of the differing meanings or associations of words. *Garden, house, plantation, gardener, estate:* these words mean one thing in England, and mean something quite different to the man from Trinidad, an agricultural colony, a colony settled for the purpose of plantation agriculture. How, then, could I write honestly or fairly if the very words I used, with private meanings for me, were yet for the reader outside shot through with the associations of the older literature? I felt that truly to render what I saw, I had to define myself as writer or narrator; I had to reinterpret things. I have tried to do this in different ways throughout my career. And after two years' work I have just finished a book in which at last – as I think – I have managed to integrate this business of reinterpreting with my narrative.

The problem that 'worried' Naipaul is a problem central to the experience of every Commonwealth writer who works in English, a language which owes its strengths and its weaknesses to Britain's expansionist, imperialistic history. Salman Rushdie made his feelings on the subject clear in a radio talk given some years ago on the BBC's Channel 4:

> Think about the ease with which the English language allows the terms of racial abuse to be coined: wog, frog, kraut, dago, spic, yid, coon, nigger, Argie. Can there be another language with so wide-ranging a vocabulary of racist denigration?

The book Naipaul wrote of as having just been finished is *The Enigma of Arrival;* in it, despite the tentativeness with which he describes his achievement, he has indeed succeeded in bringing together at last the disparate halves of both his own and the colonial experience. *Enigma* seeks to heal the division that exists between the colonial's impoverished cultural background and the richness of the literary tradition of which he desires to become a part. Readers familiar with Naipaul's work will be startled by the use of a technique new to him, in which the text casts back repeatedly over words and sentences that have been used before. It soon becomes clear that the form chosen harmonises with a central theme of change and development. The seasons as they succeed each other in the Wiltshire garden and its surrounding, certain notes that are struck in the lives of characters and in the incidents of the novel, rouse echoes of the observing writer's own experiences as a young man fresh from Trinidad twenty years before.

Like *Mr Biswas,* this new novel has its beginnings in a death, the loss of the author's younger sister who appeared in *Mr Biswas* in the fictional character of Savi, the little girl whose broken dolls' house inspires her father to construct a home of his own in which his family could live lives independent of both the charity and the ill-will of domineering relatives. We do not know of this death until we reach the last pages of the book, but long before we come upon it the succession of the seasons, the process of change and decay in the Wiltshire garden, and the difficulties of the writer's life have intimated to us that this novel is not only about arrival but about departure and death. 'My aim,' says Naipaul, 'was truth, truth to a particular experience, containing a definition of the writing self'. It is a measure of his art that when we reach the end of the book, the creative prowess itself remains as mysterious and enigmatic as ever. Like Naipaul, the reader recognises that process as a gift – 'that one of artifice one should be able to touch and stir up what is deepest in one's soul, one's heart, one's memory'!

Crow Eaters and Others

Bapsi Sidhwa, *The Crow Eaters*. 1978: rpt.
London: Jonathan Cape, 1980, pp. 283, £5.95, hardcover.

ALAMGIR HASHMI
ZURICH

Though poetry written in English in Pakistan has been a thriving art-form, novels in English are few and far between. In fact, fiction and imaginative prose as a whole have suffered an acute disfavour over the years; and while acknowledging resplendent instances of exception, such as the works of Ahmed Ali and Zulfikar Ghose, one is naturally inclined to welcome the appearance of yet another noteworthy work in the sparsely dotted landscape of prose art in our country.

The Crow Eaters, Bapsi Sidhwa's first novel, purports to be succinct and satirical account of the success story (and also related by) the Parsi Seth Faredoon Junglewalla himself, the central figure whose rise to fortune and social-stardom we follow the three hundred-odd pages strewn with matters 'local', and much good-natured humour and drollery. The speech is laconic, yet winsome as the Junglewalla tells how he pulled it off:

> Yes, I've been all things to all people in my time. There was that bumptious son-of-a-bitch in Peshawar called Colonel Williams. I cooed to him – salaamed so low I got a crick in my balls – buttered and marmalade him until he was eating out of my hand. Within a year I was handling all traffic of goods between Peshawar and Afghanistan! (p. 11)

The Parsi background and focus give additional significance to this narrative, as very little is known generally of this isolationist sort of community in the Subcontinent, particularly at a personal or imaginative level. As such, recognition of the novel's particular landscape is to register time through a consciousness with which perhaps not many outsiders would be familiar. Here is how the story finds its beginnings, from the anonymous forests of Central India to Lahore, where the Junglewallas settle down within the first twenty pages:

> Faredoon Junglewalla, Freddy for short, embarked on his travels towards the end of the nineteenth century. Twenty-three years old, strong and pioneering, he saw no future for himself in his ancestral village tucked away in the forests of central India, and resolved to seek his fortune in the hallowed pastures of the Punjab. Of the sixteen lands created by Abura Mazda and mentioned in the 4,000 year-old Vendidad, one is the 'Septa Sindu'; the Sind and Punjab of today.
>
> Loading his belongings, which included a widowed mother-in-law eleven years older than himself, a pregnant wife six years younger, and hid infant daughter Hutoxi, on to a bullock-cart, he set of North. (pp. 12–13)

We know fairly well by now the various characterisations of time through the ethnic consciousness of many of the major communities in the Sub-continent, e.g. the Muslims, Hindus, Sikhs, etc., but the present work seems to quite unique inasmuch as it permits a view of the Parsi code of feeling and behaviour. This must be the reason why the author has to continually halt the actual narrative to incorporate passages which in an academic paper would be consigned to footnotes, such as the information on Parsi customs (although some of these and a few local phrases remain unexplained) and the mode of their migration to India; or a parenthetical aside like 'Lahore can be a scold in winter as it is hot in summer) to substantiate the fact of a 'chilly afternoon' mentioned earlier in the same sentence(p. 32). This, doubtless, results in a considerable authorial presence – and perhaps gives comfort in the fact that the reader's response can only be right.

The novel has memorable characters, individual but not atypical, and of all ages, as the narrative encompasses some forty years. Gormandising Jerbanoo, Freddy's mother-in-law, is considered as his mortal foe; she manages to survive his dark plan to get rid of her setting his shop and house on fire and doubly profiting through an insurance fraud – -(a proud invention for the India of 1901, we are told in confidence) – of course the latter is a success. The heaviest weather is made in a few excremental episodes, however *true*, relating to her short visit to England where the English are exposed to Jerbanoo's Indian standards of domestic and social life. A soothsayer Fakir, a Sadhu fortune teller, a mystic, and numerous English and Indian colonial figures also make an appearance, to relieve the misery of some of the burpy, dyspeptic passages about Jerbanoo. But the dialogue for the greater remains sprightly. The story slackens after the arson episode but picks up again as the children grow up one after the other to get their chapters in. The Towers of Silence (Parsi burial grounds) provide some of the most solemn moments in the story, particularly when, contrary to Parsi tradition, as his son Soli's burial, Freddy declares the place open to outsider in a moving speech.

Regardless of the dark depths to which Freddy could stoop to stay on top, he knows how to manage himself as a Godfather of his community, to dispense favour and command, obedience and gratitude. His wife Putli (Urdu for puppet) is an ideal of Indian wifely submission, love, and responsibility. She is equally understanding towards her children, even when one of them turns out to be a poet and, later a shaven-head saint rebelling against the family tradition. The other son, Billy, comfortable 'in the proper tradition', is betrothed to lissom Tanya Easymoney, and her betrothal is 'executed with the acumen of new American cigarette being launched on the market'.

The description is always sharp-eyed. Here is Billy:

> Behram Junglewalloa, Billy for short, was a taciturn, monosyllabic, parsimonious, and tenacious little man. His tight-lipped, shrewd-eyed countenance instantly aroused mistrust – precisely because he was so trustworthy. (p. 192)

The last twist belongs to the ironical tones in which the burden of tradition id made light and bearable: 'His frugality he might have inherited from an undiluted line of Parsi forebears' (p. 192).

The 'undiluted line' plays aback on Faredoon Junglewalla's paternal lecture to Yazdi, the poet-son, who in violation of the family tradition wants to marry Rosy Watson, and Anglo-Indian classmate of doubtful respectability:

> I believe in some kind of a tiny spark that is carried from parent to child, on through generations ... a kind of inherited memory of wisdom and righteousness, reaching back to the times of Zarathustra, the Magi, the Mazdiasnians. It is tenderly nurtured conscience evolving towards perfection. (p. 129)

In a voice admirably modulated to situation, Shakespeare-quoting Freddy can as easily be the cynic of the last chapter, contemplating thus in 1940 (the date of the Pakistan Resolution passed in Lahore for the Indian-Pakistani partition and independence) the Parsi future:

> We will say where we are ... let Hindus, Muslims, Sikhs, or whosoever, rule. What does it matter? The sun will continue to rise – and the sun continue to set – in their arses ... (p. 283)

Bapsi Sidwha writes from a deep historical consciousness. Her evocation of Lahore life is lived in the first half of this century is convincing – and charming to me as a Lahorite myself. She herself grew up in Lahore and makes her home there; first-hand knowledge of it certainly lends credence to the irony, as it arises out of a deep understanding of the place and people and their ways. She is looking at the whole, and the constituent part, though the diminutive lens of insidious comicality as an insider who knows better; as a member of the Parsi minority in Pakistan who knows people's secrets, real strengths, and foibles. Her novel, beyond particular situation and character, aims at a sweep that encompasses a people and may be best considered in that light. To the small body of the fiction written in this country, Bapsi Diswha has added her witty and piquant voice and a loquaciousness that is endearing.

Gwen Harwood: Notes on The Dream

VIN BUCKLEY

It is tempting to think you know at once, at a glance, they into the matter of Gwen Harwood's poetry; for she herself has charted it, provided clue and thread; it is indicated by Wittgenstein play, language games, paintings, music. Yet this guidance may be misleading; her poems are not language games, are not notably cerebral, do not have the free-floating or teasing character of much play, and are not 'musical' in any of the more accustomed senses.

Just the same, the clues are there, and may be of use. The thing is, they have to be used in combination with other qualities, which are not mentioned so often in connection with Gwen Harwood, because they apply to so many poets. One of these is nostalgia, often dismissed as a weak emotion or state of the soul, but in Harwood's work anything but weak. She shows that there is a form of nostalgia which approximates both to the primal energies of grief and to being in love. Its keenest note is yearning, inexpressible except as a desire to recover something which has been lost, or to re-experience a long ago moment of pause and epiphany, realisation: a condition in which soul and body are stretched towards some O altitudo! That ecstatic suggestion is central to it; but so, of course, is loss. It is a remembering of things lost, for fundamentally what was possessed or felt or seen has also been lost; it has not been merely missed or foregone; and we may add to that grief as both the loss and the remembering.

Much of Gwen Harwood's poetry is suffused with this feeling; it is combined with the inseparable but still distinguishable feeling to affirm continuity by affirming the power of memory. It can do what it exists for: to make the present potent with the past.

Dust to Dust

I dream I stand once more
in Ann Street by the old
fire station. The palms
like feather dusters move
idly in stifling air.
The sky's dusted with gold.
A football; someone comes;
I cannot speak for love.
We walk in silence past
All Saints'. The dead do rise,
do live, do walk and wear
their flesh. Your exile's done.
So, so, resume our last
rejoicing kiss. Your eyes
flecked with my image stare
in wonder through my own.
Round us air turns to flame.
Ashes rain from the sky.
A fire bell clangs and clangs
insanely as I wake
to absence with your name
shaping my lips. I lie
losing the dream that hangs
fading in air. I shake
the last of night away.
These bright motes that define

morning inside my room
hold not one grain of you.
Another sunstruck day
whose moving dust-motes shine
remote from any dream
cannot restore, renew
our laughter that hot night
when by All Saints' we talked
in the brief time we had.
During the *Magnificat*
an urchin stopped to write
on the church wall. He chalked
his message: GOD IS MAD.
I say amen to that.

Here is strong ego without egotism, for the drive which forms the poem is too basic, too primal, for that; oddly enough, her speed of composition shows this; she does not allow herself time to appear to a calculated 'best advantage'; everything is gambled both on the truth of the recall and the pertinence of technique. So, too, what is affirmed is not the ego's desire to hold on but the value of the object held on to. In this case, that object is not merely and event, but a city and a young self.

I am speaking of memory raised to a creative power. It is easy to see why this complex and primal psychological state (and capacity) becomes connected with an art form: or two, or three, or four, if you count linguistic philosophy as an art-form, as it surely is. It may be less easy to see why this power is brought into the works of art (poems, memoirs, libretti, musical performances, linguistic philosophy, letters and postcards) so often through the convention of the dream, and the narrative exposition of having dreamed.

Gwen Harwood is evidently a strong dreamer and rememberer of dreams; it is interesting that the dreams which reports so precisely suit her other interests, especially her artistic and philosophical ones. It is basic to dreams *as recounted* that they are summaries, paraphrases, or scenarios, as if, after the fully filmed event, the participant audience restaged a précis of it. It also seems integral that the reported dream should be in a different mode or medium from the experienced one. Insofar as the 'public' dream is a story ('I dreamed about ...); the report is the story of a story. My daughter Grania refuses to speak as though a television program is or has a story, because for her a story is something that is told or read. But for adults a story may be also be something one acts in: for Grania, acting would be something she did 'in the real world', and not in a story. James Joyce's father had a similar view of reality: he *could not be* a character in a book, for he was here; he was not a practitioner of bi-location. The dream story may be 'remembered' as a group of several plots and diversions or divergences, or as a set of tableaux, or as a simple (if usually confusing) story-line, or as a rainbow mix of movement or impressions. What happens in the reporting of any of these is that motive is refined, rendered down, into tableau or simple movement. If once, remembered, it is recalled in formal verbal terms for the sake of the poem, if it is used to shape poems, if it has characters who speak, the refining becomes more radical still: the grief-pang and its basic motive, or its dominant motif, becomes graphic.

The dream also acts as an electrical conductor; the passionate nostalgia of the waking life passes through the dream, is re-charged there, and passes back into the waking life. Now it has all three aspects: it is an art form, it is a new conscious memory, and it is a preparedness for a new dreaming (obviously, one can come to experience nostalgia for a dream state. If all this takes place in a person who, far from being cut off from ordinary affairs and pushed towards the silliness of constant reverie, lives very much in the ordinary world and in touch with world affairs, it may not be the reference I need (do I in fact mean syncopation?), but it does seem that a musical, not a painterly analogue is called for. Life becomes modelled on music, through dream.

If dreams are an art-form, they are one practised chiefly by bunglers. I am one such, a bad dreamer in more than one sense: the dreams often stifle me, I can remember them, and never try to report them. Yet they are proper dreams; their overt meaning is thick, comprehensible, and lacking in clues which I feel any anxiety about decoding. I am also a poor letter-writer. Gwen Harwood is a good dreamer, that is, she shapes the dream in recall so as to get to its thematic core very easily. This core is not necessarily what the analyst would get from it (the motive, as it were), but the thing which accretes and carries its feeling (the motif). It may be no accident that, as well as being a musician, she is a splendid writer of letters and postcards. In each of these art forms there is a principle of psychic economy at work; life, art, and dream all change one another.

We may see in her example, then, the following things:

> The dream is art: not high art or low art, but deep art.
> Its lights and darknesses are more pressing than others.
> But the poem 'about' a dream is not a dream but a poem.
> The form recounting the dream is not a dream-matter but language waiting to be connected (corrected?)
> The real place and the dream place are of equal vividness but different sizes.
> Dreams are now like films; before the era of films they were like formal essays in confession.
> Now we see dreams as showing how things diverge; for Freud and Jung they showed how things converge.

But I go too far; I know nothing about these things, which furthermore are not the business of a bad dreamer. I am on the verge of playing language games, of a sort which takes me further away from both music and dreams. My motives in this are suspect. Gwen Harwood would never dream of such thing.

She does, however, make these associations clearly *in her poems*; and she does so increasingly in her later work, *The Lion's Bride*:

I am curved, a shadow in crystal,
and cannot break through to the world,
so reach for my one drug, music,
and turn it on. It's Caruso.
He is singing *M'appari.*
Well, let life imitate art.
A tenor sings, 'like a dream',
and a woman sits still and listens.
I feel the drug take hold
of my body, a lover's touch,
as I stare bemused at the fire
and hear the soft rustle of coals
orange hot from the heart of some tree
in a dialogue of passion
darkening, descending to charcoal.
('Diotima')

Each theme, each motif, joins its partners as though, an act of art being begun, they could not fail to do so. This is not because of any routinism in the psychic process; and she is certainly not playing, language or any other games. It is rather that in her mental world they *belong* together. We can also see an argument might be mounted to show that mental world is normative for psychic life, and central to civilisation: music, life-art, dream, woman, drug, body, lover,; and although this is by no means Harwood at her finest, we see that the associational chain works to bring her into the world from where she is 'curved, a shadow in crystal'. It releases her, that is. The world into which she comes is the poem, thus adding the final term in the sequence. And so beginning the cycle again, which will lead by some free logic to music, dream, and body.

What consent do we ever
give to dreams that embrace us
with the energy of art?
Why do you come at morning

when frosty air is burning
my empty arms? I split
wood, light the day's fire,
warm my body at flame
invisible in sunlight.
That brief motto in Latin,
on what door was it written?
Tell me, what is your name?
('Oyster Cove Pastorals')

The answer to the last question is in the stanzas which introduce it. Which suggests that, for Gwen Harwood as for many other artists, waking dream and sleeping dream are shades on each other: given that the word 'dream' for these conditions and experiences must seem to many critics old-fashioned and romantic. 'Dreaming's an art. Dreams can be recreated'. But that's the beginning of the problem: Can they? It seems from common practice that they cannot be replicated, although I have met people who have asserted convincingly that they can be *retrieved* after being lost. Poetry's an art, too but what would it mean to say that poems can be recreated? We know it is very difficult even to translate or paraphrase them. I think Gwen Harwood is referring to something which we express by speaking of 'calling up' a thought, a person, or an experience: something akin to necromancy.

At any rate, this calling-up acts in Gwen Harwood's poetry not to lengthen language games, but to straighten out story and feeling. Hers is a very direct art; and except in the Kröte and Eisenbart poems, and a few others, play does not seem its object. Perhaps play is its premise; perhaps the play takes place at the point where the poem effectively begins. In the Kröte poems, to play is to play music: pieces of music, or a music. In other poems, like 'Dust to Dust', the lyric engages in a form of dance. Is dancing playing? Is dance a game? Or may it be the completion of a game?

The finest poems in *The Lion's Bride* and afterwards seem to me to go far beyond the condition of 'lyric', in form or in feeling. One such is 'Dialogue', a poem of recall in which nevertheless the poet keeps firm control of the terms on which the recall is to occur:

> If an angel came with one wish
> I might say, deliver that child
> who died before birth, into life.
> Let me see what she might have become.
> He would bring her into a room
> fair skinned   the bones of her hands
> would press on my shoulderblades
> in one long embrace
>   we would sit
> with the albums spread on our knees:
> now here are your brothers   and here
> your sister ...

As it goes on, this beautiful and very moving poem replaces dream with vision, and play with dialectic: a Socratic opening up of the fields where they toil not, and memory delivers the very heartbeat of the present.

The Heart

ANNE BREWSTER
UNIVERSITY OF WESTERN SYDNEY

I feel and watch. The way sound from the cars or the planes overhead rattles round a room. The way a woman's red lipstick frames her words and people's brows shine with perspiration. The way the day pauses between meetings. Speaking is like sweeping paths or the scaffolding round a building. Leaves gather again, grass grows between the cracks. The scaffolding is assembled and disassembled; the house shines with its new coat of paint. Feelings roost in the heart, the skin. I can't step outside the skin although I've wanted to fold it like a blanket at the end of the bed. The heart like a furrowed field, splinters of wood, wire. The heart like a tv screen, filled with noise, movement. It holds the face of the dead man, the rows of numbers, the images of that country far away yet close. Nothing will stop. Every moment something emerges from the frozen surface of things. In the pit of the stomach I feel my human self. And admiring the body which continues in spite of everything. The novelist told me that he spent the whole book planning the ending. If the end is theatre, what is the working up to the end? I watch him but I'm really watching myself. In yoga they say that we forget the back of the body and the weight of what we can't see. I never did understand how to simply leave it there.

Static or Grunge Revisited

RON BLABER
CURTIN UNIVERSITY

Margaret Thatcher famously or infamously once suggested that there was no such thing as society, there were only families and individuals. As we will see a later, even the 'existence' of families becomes problematic. But to a certain degree such beliefs can be associated with the emergence of post-modern or post-civil social formations. The utterance underpinned a form of aspiration that focussed on a type of wealth generation that was selfish and socially divisive. It was further fuelled by an abundance of easy access to credit and by a boom in property values, against which further credit became available. This of course was unsustainable. The Global Financial Crisis of 2007-08 followed by questions of sovereign debt in the Eurozone undid the aspirationalism associated with the restructuring of the economy initiated by the policies of governments headed by the likes of Thatcher, Reagan, and Hawke/Howard.

In 2011 England was beset with riots: no place more so than in London. The Cameron government was quick to condemn the rioters as criminals and set in place draconian and mandatory processes to ensure the perpetrators were arrested tried, convicted and imprisoned. There were a number of reasons for the haste. The government of the day, as a tenuous coalition, needed to look decisive; the government of the day needed to ensure that an any analogies to the Arab spring were quickly negated; with the 2012 Olympics just over the horizon, London need to look safe and friendly. The Government was ably assisted by a media equally committed to casting the riots as criminal in nature and worse suggesting the rioters were possible victims of an activist conspiracy. Nevertheless, and not surprisingly, a counter discourse emerged and continues to hold some influence. Here it was argued that the riots had there basis in the social and economic restructuring that had held sway for the past three decades. In effect, the argument suggests the legacy of neoliberal market economics instigated by the Reagan and Thatcher governments was one in which society was increasingly marked by a radical difference between the 'haves' and 'have-nots;' that there was an increasing number of individuals and families who were excluded from a consumerist polity. If this were the case then the riots can be read as a lagging effect of the Global Financial Crisis, the government response to which was to bail out the financial institutions whose practices had brought on the GFC rather than support those most immediately effected. The GFC and the riots were a long time in the making but devastating in their consequences. In the background to these events there had emerged discussion about the making or re-energising of the 'Big Society.' In essence the 'Big Society' is envisaged as a form of collectivism and volunteerism which was held to always be there as a basis of community and society but had been diminished under neoliberal economic practices. Nevertheless, it also came to be felt that if this principles could be energised, then not only could community be re-established, it could also lead to 'small government,' that is to say government services could be transferred to forms of collectivism and volunteerism. In other words we are looking at a refashioning of the social.

Curiously, the potential for refashioning underlies much of grunge narrative. This essay returns to an earlier moment, one that might be considered central to the event, when it occurred, of the GFC, that is the moment when in the late 70s early 80s when western Governments moved quickly to a neoliberal free market economic policy. Early impacts were wages contraction, attacks on unions and spikes in youth unemployment. And one of the early consequences was the making of a new underclass.

Within such a context how can people fashion their own agency amid an increasingly messy social structure. The problematic for this paper is that literary studies, and its associated interpretive strategies are imbricated in a modernist project within which operates a progressive view of the formation of the social and the articulation of individual identity. At issue then is how literary studies, with its modern history, positions itself within the post-civil. Here grunge is offered as a case study. The case study is grounded in two considerations: Grunge and its interpretation; the relationship between grunge and agency.

We understand the term 'grunge' was appropriated from its musical origins in the nineties by the publishing industry in Australia and applied to a new urban literature. Regardless of protestations, grunge is used to describe the fiction of Justine Ettler, Edward Berridge, Christos Tsiolkas, Clare Mendes and Andrew McGahan amongst others. Ian Syson argues the generalised use of the term was primarily about producing a new reading market with the revitalisation of OZlit as a secondary concern. However, Syson suggests there is a commonality of protest operating in grunge fiction and offers an interpretive strategy aligning it with a particular tradition of Australian writing.

Nevertheless, if grunge could be generalised as a style I suggest it is a form of hyper-realism marked by extensive and intensive description of youthful demotic lifestyles, predominantly but not exclusively male with emphasis being placed on sex, drugs, the delinquent if not outright criminal, and pathological boredom. Edward Berridge says of his writing: 'For me, for now it's all to do with the thrill, regular shots of sex and violence to counter low thresholds of boredom' (15). Nevertheless a significant number of grunge texts display traces of modernism, for example the narrative voices in *Praise* and *Drift Street* owe a great deal to confessional and epiphanic modes of narrative. For example, the narrative technique employed in Clare Mendes's *Drift Street* owes more to Faulkner than to the Seattle scene. And the theme of Justine Ettler's *The River*

Ophelia locates and binds within a Sadean/Bataillean tradition. If we accept the above description of grunge, then I would argue the term can be applied to a number of literary and filmic texts. There are obvious connections to the writings of Irvine Welsh (*Trainspotting*) and Joseph O'Connor (*Cowboys and Indians*) and to films, in which grunge seems to have had a longer life, such as *Romper Stomper*, *Metal Skin*, *Shopping*, *Go*, *Two Hands*, *The Boys*, and *Sample People*.

Further and importantly, it should come as no surprise that for the most part grunge has been interpreted in terms of alienation and abjection. These strategies locate grunge within a Marxist or psychoanalytic frame recuperating these representations to a modernist concern with the relationship between the individual and self, but generally in an apolitical context in so far as most of the texts are marked by a 'middleclasslessness.' And central to nearly all of the readings of these texts is a concern with the self-fashioning of an identity in light of the collapse of social institutions traditionally underpinning such a process – gone are the family, school, the workplace. For the most part disappearance is read as loss. Any economic structure tends to be that of the black market and the criminal. Solutions put in place by the state to function as safety nets, such as out-reach programs or drop-in centres, are under stress and are more concerned with budgetary bottom-lines. Julian, the drop-in centre manager in Berridge's 'Bored Teenagers,' has to battle zoning regulations to keep operating in the face of residents' complaints. 'But it is all bullshit, like everything Julian ever says and no-one pays attention to him' (1).

However, if disappearance appears to be much more than loss or absence, then disappearance becomes a 'way-down-an-out.' The opening paragraph of Edward Berridge's *Lives of the Saints* captures something of the flavour:

> Everyone is bored. Bored, bored fucking bored. Dennis sits with his feet up on the table, Albert lounges over by the Cafe

> Bar, Farrah smokes another cigarette. One more night. Kylie plays aimlessly with the radio dial trying to find something cool but there is nothing but shit and the reception is too bad to tolerate anyway. She says, you know what we need? You know what we really need? But no one responds. She says, we need a CD player and some CDs. (1)

We are too familiar, perhaps with the image of the 'Bored Teenager.' As something of an icon of Australian Grunge realism, the 'bored teenager' is also a hypermediatised image – cliché-ed and wired to youth suicide, shooting galleries, mandatory sentencing, welfare – areas where the state seeks to assert itself through regulation or exhortation to charitable services. Important in Berridge's description is not so much the boredom but the absence of connection and reception (Kylie 'plays aimlessly with the radio dial'). These lives are beset with noise, ('the reception is too bad to tolerate anyway'). Their conversation is not signalled as speech – there are no quotation marks used – and they are effectively voiceless. The CD player, a significant consumer item, is not within their world. These are not teenage consumers, a category emerging in the fifties and powering on ever since; these are not the nightmare teenagers of middle-class dysfunctional family sitcoms or horror flicks. Worse. The image of the bored teenager marks the border between the civil and the post-civil, resisting but inviting modernist paradigms of interpretation and recuperation.

Berridge's postmodernist performance is a flirtation with the post – civil, emphasising surface over depth, the ephemeral over value. Berridge does not iterate the modern concern of alienation, rather he identifies noise and spaces that are set out of place, created as consequences of a shift in the formation of the social: the sign of grunge; a sign of the post-civil.

The style/form called grunge realism is a part of and an attempt to represent aspects of fashioning a sense of identity and agency. The exploration of grunge realism is prompted by the following passage from Joseph O'Connor's *Cowboys and*

Indians and the passage is viewed as providing a way of reading a range of texts.

> Eddie leaned over till his head was right between his knees and he puked up like a fruit machine. He gawked up steaming vomit all over his chinos and his new Doc Martens, and when he clamped his mouth shut, puke oozed from his nostrils. Sweat soaked through his forehead. Puke gulped through his tightened lips. His spit was thick and ropey as he spat. Puke dribbled down his chin and dripped into his pocket of his shirt. He slithered down on all fours and puked even harder, and his puke splashed all over the girl's feet and his fingers. And the sound of his puke, splashing on the floor, made him want to puke again. (10)

The passage juxtaposes style with a betrayal of that style. In one sense the self-fashioning, self-defining aspect of style is undermined by a fundamental excess, or in Kristevan terms a moment of abjection in which self and other become interfused, the markers of identity and non-identity become blurred. Kristeva argues the case that certain narratives re-story the formation and construction of identity, 'the adolescent again questions his identifications, along with his capacities for speech and symbolisation' (9). However, this moment permits the possibility of a new self-fashioning. What is important then, regardless of the relationship between style and identity, signified by clothing or the gestural, identity, as an aspect of the corporeal signified by the abject, is reduced to the infantile, if not the primordial. Regression of this type appears characteristic of what has been termed grunge realism and provides another foundation for refiguring the identity.

However before moving on to textual analysis the term Grunge realism needs interrogation. Generally speaking the term lacks categorical specificity but as a consequence manifests a provocative and productive power in so far as it is operates within the space created by the dynamic relationship between the critical and seductive. In other words there is something we find desirable in the 'idea' of grunge realism. It captures an opportunity and a promise of the autopoetic, a chance to refashion the self, or perhaps institutions and traditions. Style is both a form of autopoesis and sociopoesis. It functions as a form of self-fashioning, a means of differentiating oneself from others within the broader community and as a means of identifying with possible like-minded others. However, style stands in a determining relationship with hegemonic interpellative processes. In other words, style functions oppositionally. Dick Hebdige reads style 'as a form of Refusal' (2) and argues that 'Refusal is worth making ... even if, in the final analysis [it is] just the darker side of sets of regulations ...' (3). It is also a way of countering fear. Nevertheless style as oppositional or subversive becomes further radicalised under conditions in which the hegemonic begins to lose its broad power. Style gives way to something else, a more radical autopoesis figured in a blurring of boundaries, sometimes in the unsettling of the somatic – the realm of the abject. Thus once the hegemonic is diminished, style becomes both less and more significant, as the abject comes into play.

The extensive and intensive descriptions underscore grunge realism's concern with struggles over fashioning identity, a process of autopoesis, not always successful, but figured in the relationship between style and abjection.

To say that grunge realism is about autopoesis is trite. One could argue that all narrative is about autopoesis, but I argue a specificity for the struggle for identity, for self-fashioning that occurs within grunge and this struggle is represented by a range of hyper-real and surreal strategies.

I take my understanding of autopoesis from Felix Guattari's theory of resingularisation of subjectivity. Singularity refers to a point that supports and confirms subjectivity. New experiences or contradictions that both fix and disrupt that node may produce a resingularisation. The opportunity for resingularisation can be determined by factors outside of regulatory discourses or what may be described in Foucauldian terms as non-discursive; or perhaps produced through the clash or contradictions between regulatory discourses; or, perhaps in psychoanalytic terms, the effects of the prelinguistic within the symbolic.

As mentioned earlier, what is significant about the relationship between style and abjection within grunge narratives is the failure or diminution of regulatory processes that underpin hegemonic subjectivities and identities. For example, place has traditionally functioned to provide a grounding for identity, but in O'Connor's *Cowboys and Indians* place is one of those traditional supports that fails. The novel is set in London and Ireland. We discover from the narrator's point of view that Ireland has become a place of 'sentimental maudlin love songs and country and western standards. All broken promises, wayward rovers, lonesome cowboys' (13); Ballybracken is figured as not quite part of the late twentieth century, the 'kind of place where you plug in an electric toothbrush and the streetlights dim'(4); England is corrupt and decaying with London seen as 'the eye of the storm, the rotten apple, the monstrous and fetid birthplace of punk' (2); and postindustrial Birmingham becomes Yeats's 'rough beast, come to life in the flat and lifeless heartland of England' (13). In Andrew McGahan's *Praise* subjectivity is most clearly defined by the bureaucratic requirements of the Department of Social Security which provides a governmental identity but in a time of recession the DSS represents the last vestige of one's citizenship. In the Geoffrey Wright's film *Metal Skin*, family no longer functions to provide a secure individual or social identity: Joe's father suffers dementia to the detriment of Joe's socialisation; Safina's mother is obsessively tidy, overbearingly religious, and Safina responds through a messy, bloody satanic inversion. This is furthered underscored the respective homes. Both are cavernous and oppressive; one is dark, chaotic and apparently verminous; the other bright, spotless and sterile.

The family is similarly absent in Paul Anderson's *Shopping* Authority is represented by a pressurised police force beset and attacked by a criminal and criminalised underclass and yet is reliant on one criminal betraying another in order to do its job. The main character is caught in a permanent childhood. Billy, 19, just released from prison responds to the question 'Why don't you grow up?' by saying 'And do what?'

The question 'And do what?' is a further characteristic of grunge realism. The absence or failure of traditional structures of identity which in turn provide the basis for productive life leads to boredom and meaningless activity, the ingredients of what appears to be a pathological ennui. To do something may indeed be a way of finding or making oneself but there is nothing out there but static. However for the most part, and not surprisingly, self-fashioning occurs through relationship. And in the world of grunge realism the fashioning of an identity through the intersubjective is fraught given that in a consumerist society, which reduces subjects to isolated monads, relationship no longer functions as foundational of identity. Rather at the heart of relationship is an existential aloneness. Nevertheless it remains one site of resingularisation.

In both O'Connor's *Cowboys and Indians* and McGahan's *Praise* the protagonists attempt to confirm a sense of identity through relationships increasingly reduced to sexual activity rather than through love or even friendship. Furthermore, sex becomes a site of fragmentation. Eventually relationships collapse, symptomatic of a broader social fragmentation.

Loneliness is the dominant tenor of *Cowboys and Indians*. At the end of the novel Eddie leaves Marion, continues to drift and in that drifting he comments on a minor symptom of consumerism. He notes that Christmas lights are going up in October and that 'they'd put the lights up a little early one year, and leave them up a little late,' (250). We get a sense of boundaries dissolving. Eddie thinks:

> One of these years it would end up being Christmas all the time ... The definitions that keep things apart would just disappear. It had to happen. (250)

Ironically, Eddie has no-one with which to share his observation, but within that observation there lies a point of resingularisation, an opportunity self-refashioning. A similar moment occurs at the conclusion of McGahan's *Praise*. Needless to say Gordon's relationships fail and he might be said to fail in fashioning a new identity, in so far as he remains protean, being more in flux than in formation. At the end of the novel, he arrives at a point of awareness if not transformation. He tells us:

> I looked around the flat. I thought about things. It was almost nine months since I'd been employed. Did I want to go back? Was this life working or wasn't it?
>
> I didn't know any more. The old certainty was gone.
>
> But a job, a job? Surely work wasn't the answer. Things weren't going to well for me at the moment, but surely the rest of society didn't have it right either, did they? (278)

Gordon's question is a crucial one for a number of reasons. It is representative of a number of grunge realist narratives, again in relation to hegemonic processes, but more significantly it is an address to the reader that emerges from a narrative voice which is problematically at once confessional and self-ironising. The tone, then, underscores grunge, a questioning of normative processes which otherwise is diminished in other narrative modes. However, how do *Cowboys and Indians* and *Praise* reach this point?

As we have noted earlier, Eddie Virago, the protagonist of the *Cowboys and Indians*, is characterised as existing in a blur of the stylish and the abject. However, Eddie Virago's ambitions provide some refuge from a world that again provides no guarantees of subjectivity or identity. Because of his rock'n'roll dreams, Eddie engages in differences in style but is caught between his good looks and his function as a late punk tourist attraction. Nevertheless, underlying Eddie's superficiality is an existential aloneness. We are told:

> Eddie Virago was alone, just him and his guitar and his ego. And at twenty-four, you don't worry too much about that. It's exciting to be alone. You don't know what being alone is, not yet, but it's a big deal to you and that's something. (1)

Through the course of the narrative, however, the connection between self and loneliness becomes increasingly significant and is most acutely figured through Eddie's relationship with Marion. Rather than confirming an identity, relationship exacerbates Eddie's sense of loneliness, which in turn threatens any sense of self that he may have. While acknowledging a love for Marion, Eddie feels it to be a threat to his being yet paradoxically there is no solidity to that being. At the same time in the background there lies the abject signified by a primal fear, a sense of collapse and enervation.

> And the moment Eddie looked at her, he knew he was in love.
>
> It was a pain in the ass but he knew he couldn't stop gazing at her ... Eddie recognised all the signs. The same primal terror, the same sense of things falling around him and the doors opening in his head, the same sense of torpid inevitability, they were all there and it was the damn same. (84)

In Guattari's terms, the opportunity for resingularisation is held in abeyance by repetitive behaviours constituting an impasse. We get an understanding to this process early in the novel and yet there is a suggestion of moving beyond the impasse couched in terms of a vague longing:

> The very thing he'd promised himself he wouldn't do – get tied up with somebody too quickly – and now he'd done it. This had all the potential of a real Torvil and Dean situation. Thin ice all round, and Eddie could already feel it beginning to crack ...

> ... he lay there very still beside her, wondering why this had happened, and how he was going to get out of it. He felt a hollow feeling deep inside the very core of his existence. But it wasn't emotion. It was hunger. (30–1)

Hunger and loneliness become the problematic of the novel and are very much tied to issues of self-fashioning. Eddie does not want to understand sex outside of some fleeting personal satisfaction but even that is challenged by a representation of female sexuality that has a voracious and fundamental reality to it and yet seems fictional and escapist. Eddie's confusion leads to a further sense of loneliness:

> Marion wanted to do it in positions that Eddie has only ever read about. She fucked him hard like there was just no point to what they were doing, no reason at all, except the essential longing for some sort of escape. And the weirdest thing of all was that when he touched her body she said 'Oh baby' and 'Baby, that's good' in an attempt at a languid growl that just sounded so utterly out of character it made Eddie wonder what the fuck was going on. She sounded like a character in some cheap 1970s airport novel.
>
> And when she came she wrenched something out of herself, from deep down, and winced silently as though she was in agony. And when Eddie came he clutched at the bedspread and felt lonelier than he'd ever thought possible. (21–2)

Paradoxically, the physicality of sex becomes alienating rather than an intimate part of relationship. Furthermore sexual activity escalates in a desperate bid to overcome the alienation and abjection that it engenders. This story is repeated in McGahan's *Praise*.

For Gordon, the 23-year-old narrator of *Praise*, style is not really an issue unless one describes a pervasive sense of ennui as a style. Within that ennui there is a sense of the abject underlying relationship and sex. Sex is a mystery for Gordon. He is aware that sex is intricately woven into the construction a normative masculine identity but his experience constantly falls short of that identity. He tells us:

> Most of my friends came from other parts of my life. From School. University. Most of the sex came from there too, but there wasn't that much sex and what there was hadn't been much good. I was young and nervous and not very enthusiastic. I didn't have the libido I felt I was supposed to have. And I didn't expect things to improve. I relied on masturbation. (7)

And

> My body was the problem. My prick had no guts. It couldn't take over my brain like pricks were supposed to. (19)

Gordon's experience of sex, then, is figured not only in terms inadequacy but also terms of a problematic corporeality. His body is not what it should be in ideological terms. His body does not provide the ground for individual, social or gender identity. In one sense Gordon fails to enter the symbolic. On looking in mirror Gordon sees himself as incoherent: 'I was pale and round and unshaven, with a head of long tangled hair. Not even enough fat there to look sleek. Just flab. What was the appeal' (48). And to a degree sex, which supposedly represents the body at its most bodily, erases any sense of being. Of his sexual relationship with Cynthia, Gordon states:

> It depressed me. I was beginning to suspect that Cynthia's orgasms came not so much from anything *I* did as from her ability to turn herself on to things, to anything, and anyone. I could've *been* anyone. Maybe that was the way it would always be with sex, and maybe there was nothing surprising about it, but I felt the needed to do something more. I had to prove my existence. I needed power. I rolled her over again and applied my mouth to her clitoris. (44)

and later;

> And I was coming too fast. Or not coming at all. Always at the wrong times. Cynthia didn't mind so much. My body wasn't going anywhere. She knew she could get whatever she

> wanted from it in time. But it bothered me. It was even harder to get imaginative with a prick that you couldn't rely on. (89)

Implicit within Gordon's description here is the belief that by contrast Cynthia has some control some clearer sense of identity. He regards Cynthia's body as 'solid and strong and indulgent'(48). Ironically, her body, at least the dermis, is falling apart, ravaged by allergies. Furthermore she too looks for confirmation of identity through sex:

> If she could fuck, she was alive.
> I did my best.
> I appreciated the philosophy. (189)

If sex and the body cannot confirm any sense of identity or subjectivity, it is not surprising then that relationship does not work. Where relationship, the construction of subjectivity through intersubjectivity, should provide a foundation for identity, we find alienation, disjunction and boredom. Gordon's empty self-obsession (being full of not himself) prevents any connection with Cynthia:

> I looked up at her. It was not a thing I understood. I had no sense of timing, of when things should or shouldn't be happening in a relationship. Or when a relationship had even started. (17)

Furthermore, lack of connection represents a lack or an inability for intimacy makes Gordon view of his relationship with Cynthia grotesque:

> We kissed.
>
> There was no emotion in it. My eyes were open and staring at her face. Our mouths were stretched, our tongues jamming in and out. It was grotesque. I was not fond of kissing. Either it was like this, grotesque, or it was something terribly tender. Something far more than sex, something that demanded sincerity. And I had real problems with sincerity. (19)

In both *Cowboys and Indians* and *Praise*, then, the diminution of the power of social structures undermines normative subjective processes and identity formation. Sex is not sufficient to take the place of those social structures and indeed rather than providing a foundation for identity formation it becomes alienating and abject. The tentative realisation that sex is symptomatic of greater social fragmentation, however, allows Eddie and Gordon opportunities for resingularisation. The film texts I now investigate are less optimistic.

In terms of film, the examination of the interplay of the autopoetic, style and abjection becomes a little more complex in so far as realism a dominant mode of representation which constrains the type of interplay evident in the novels. Therefore the term grunge realism may be inappropriate term, and perhaps we need to consider the possibility of grunge surrealism or grunge expressionism both of which could incorporate the abject. This seems to be the case with *Metal Skin* and *Shopping*, however, in both films the abject is figured less in sexuality and more through the individual's relationship to a decaying social and cultural environment.

Geoffrey Wright's *Metal Skin* might be categorised as grunge in so far as it is marked by signs common to the narrative mode. It is set against a claustrophobic society figured by youth unemployment, dead end jobs and a post-industrial landscape of dock and rail yards. Patriarchal and therefore social authority, through and against which identity is formed, is noticeably absent. And in Joe's case this absence is clearly signalled by his mentally ill father. Style is centred on marginally criminal activity of drag racing, the races subject to police raids. Cars are illegally modified. Those with the best looking and fastest cars are the most admired. For the most part the character Daisy is top of the social hierarchy, however, his reputation is marred having had a serious accident. The newcomer is Joe, a social misfit. And if a car can signify the abject, his does: the rear view mirror keeps dropping off; the tyres are balding; the rear spoiler threatens to come off; its black duco needs repainting. Of all the characters going nowhere, Joe is most likely to succeed, tragically so.

To underscore the individual and social fragmentation central to the film, the editing is non-realistic. Time and space are blurred in accord with fragmentation of the social. Narrative is non-linear, mixing flashback, flash forward and the present. Sequences are marked by a staccato editing disrupting any linear development. However the film is anchored in so far as we are told the action takes place in Melbourne in 1994.

The film opens with a high pitched sound, possibly a woman's scream; possibly the scrape of metal against metal. The ambiguity characterises the film and sets in place the problem of definitions keeping things apart. The focus of the film is the interactions of the characters Robert Day, (whose masculinity is diminished through his nickname – Daisy), Ros, Safina, and Joe. All are damaged individuals literally and metaphorically; their bodies and psychologies are marked by the abject. Daisy appears the most stable but is alienated from his father and brother; he is sexually promiscuous but this 'just happens'; and he is guilt stricken by the injuries he caused Ros in a car crash. Ros is badly disfigured, her breasts and abdomen badly burnt, her femininity destroyed. Safina has suffered leukemia, lives at home with an obsessive mother, and in reaction Safina becomes a witch as a way of achieving what she wants in the world, which amounts to a relationship with Daisy. Joe, sometimes called crazy Joe, is on medication for epilepsy which he takes with alcohol in order to cope with his isolation brought about by caring for his father who suffers from dementia. Each seeks to restore a sense of social and individual identity through relationship with one or two of the other characters. However, the relationships among the characters are destructive as their desires are never achieved. For example Joe seeks friendship with Daisy and love with Safina; Safina seeks friendship with Joe and love with Daisy; Daisy wants to be friends with everyone and to be forgiven by Ros.

The most important relationship is between Joe and Daisy. It repeats the classic construction of Australian mateship figured against stereotypic ethnic sub-cultures which seem to control the illegal drags. However, the mateship is also classically undermined through Joe's and Daisy's rivalry for the love of Safina and Ros. The final confrontation between Joe and Daisy, however, hesitantly re-appropriates traditional subjectivities if in tragic circumstances. They are involved in a high speed duel, resulting in Joe's death. Joe's death can be read as the containment of the abject in so far has he has stood in chaotic opposition to Daisy. After the duel Daisy asserts unconvincingly 'I beat you! I beat you!' Ros, who has accompanied Daisy, disappears among the containers in the dock yards, literally withdrawing into a metal skin.

Paul Anderson's *Shopping* is almost old fashioned, Dickensian with a techno-industrial soundtrack. It represents Britain in terms of a divided nation; a wealthy powerful invisible upper class, and a visible, disempowered underclass, existing in yet another post-industrial landscape of abandoned factories and decaying housing estates. *Shopping* represents a paranoid social structure in which the autopoetic, resingularisation is severely limited. While traditional supports for identity formation appear not to be functioning and the world has become divided between fortress consumerism and criminal underclass, with the latter laying siege to the former. The film is concerned with the fight for survival within that underclass and the two main combatants are Billy and Tommy, who have been rivals for most of their lives. Billy remains locked in an ultimately destructive adolescence, while Tommy begins to establish a criminal network: drugs, car theft, black-market goods. On the one hand Billy continues to function at the level of male adolescent bravado. When asked what he learned in prison Billy replies 'Don't get caught.' On the other hand Tommy recognises the political reality of surviving within a criminal and criminalised underclass.

Shopping – ram raiding, 'crash and carry' – underscores Billy and Tommy's rivalry. Shops like the Alaska, malls like Retailland represent the consumerist culture from which Billy and Tommy are excluded. In one sense they are consigned to an abject world. Billy in his ramshackle and chaotic caravan has no hope of legitimating participating in the luxury that is the dominant feature of consumerism. Tommy operating from out an underground warren of a 'hideout' regards these shops as a natural resource which he mines to supply a black-market. Billy goes shopping just to show he can do it; Tommy goes shopping to make money. Billy, in order to prove he is the best, continually frustrates Tommy's plans. Finally, Tommy, having become aware of Billy's plans to raid Retailland, informs the police. Billy, Jo, Bebop and Monkey are killed during the raid.

Just prior to the raid, Jo, would-be girlfriend to Billy, tries to persuade him to give up his obsession of proving that he is better than Tommy and to leave. However, Billy is unable to see beyond his immediate circumstance, locked into style that no longer works;

> Jo: Let's just go.
> Billy: Can't do that.
> Jo: Look around you Billy. You've got nothing left here. Nothing to stay for.
> Billy: What's the point. There's nothing better than this. This is my home.

For Billy there is no growing up; there is no possibility to leave home. And for Tommy identity remains locked into the stereotypic relationship between a criminal underclass and a pressurised police force. Billy's death, as with Joe's in *Metal Skin*, represents a containment of the abject.

In one sense the texts examined here represent aspects of postmodernism or late capitalism. On the one hand the apparent lessening of hegemonic power offers the opportunity for the autopoetic by allowing the abject to prove productive yet, paradoxically, on the other hand the texts remind readers of how hegemonic processes operate to restore power but not necessarily within the same regulatory frameworks.

Texts cited

Edward Berridge, *The Lives of the Saints*, St Lucia: University of Queensland Press, 1995.

Justine Ettler, *The River Ophelia*, Sydney: Picador, 1995.

Andrew McGahan, *Praise*, Sydney: Allen & Unwin, 1995.

Clare Mendes, *Drift Street*, Sydney: Harpers Collins, 1995.

Joseph O'Connor, *Cowboys and Indians*, London: Flamingo, 1992.

Irvine Welsh, *Trainspotting*, London: Secker and Warburg, 1993.

Shopping, Dir. Paul Anderson, 1993.

Two Hands, Dir. Gregor Jordan, 1999.

Go, Dir. Doug Liman, 1999.

Sample People, Dir. Clinton Smith, 2000.

Metal Skin, Dir. Geoffrey White, 1994.

Romper Stomper, Dir. Geoffrey White, 1992.

The Boys, Dir. Rowan Woods, 1998.

Felix Guattari, *Chaosmosis: An Ethico-aesthetic Paradigm*, trans. Paul Bains and Julian Pefanis, Sydney: Power Publications, 1995.

Dick Hebdige, *Subculture: The Meaning of Style*, London: Methuen, 1979.

Julia Kristeva, 'The Adolescent Novel,' in *Abjection, Melancholia and Love: The Work of Julia Kristeva*, eds. John Fletcher and Andrew Benjamin, London: Routledge, 1990.

Ian Syson, 'Smells Like Market Spirit,' *Overland*, 142, 1996

Murray Waldren, 'Lit. Grit Invades OzLit,' *The Australian Magazine*, June, 1995.

Odysseus, My Father

SUDESH MISHRA

UNIVERSITY OF MELBOURNE

'Bring sulfur, nurse, to scour all pollution –
Bring me fire too, so I can fumigate the house.'
The Odyssey, trans. Robert Fagles

After twenty years of fruit picking, factory work, he steps out of a rundown ford, casual as yesterday.

Gift-free, guiltless, he explains nothing, makes no fuss.

His first act – to shoo me out, wing down doors, windows, punish the house with brimstone, set a great dragon breathing through bedroom and closet, through the cracks and webs of his long vacancy.

Meanwhile, I stand on the edge of a crater, fuming, fume-drunk, wonderstruck at the stranger's cheek.

I shall doubt all his stories: how, shipwrecked, he played gigolo to a sexed-up nymph; how, lashed to the mainmast, he outfoxed a squad of sly sopranos; blinding a bung-eyed monster, how he upset the wine-dark seas; and this I shall mistrust the most, how he nattered with grandma's ghost in some moth-balled necropolis.

But he keeps it straight, tenders no excuse.

A shoestring fare, a cut-prize jet, a polite vegan crew, and, presto, he was home and hosed.

Now, as we pile up the corpses of slain suitors – roaches, spiders, moths – inside the chicken coop, I clean forget to tell him of mother, dead ten years at the loom.

Rite of Spring: A Night Out in Sachsenhausen

BRIAN MATTHEWS
FLINDERS UNIVERSITY

Wednesday, 25 March: evening

Not spring yet, and certainly not in Frankfurt where the locals keep apologising for the city's glass-and-gleam anonymity and where two or three seasons battle each other through every day. Mostly, there is wind-drifted sleet, or rain cold and whippy, but today – today has been different. Everyone notices, coming on to the street for the first time that morning: the air mellow, the light in a high, white sky seeming not of the sun. By mid-morning patches of glittering blue are gaping in the luminous brightening overcast. People carry their overcoats and if you walk briskly you perspire.

A foretaste of spring. No hope of its lasting long but darkness seems only to intensify the mellow atmosphere and people flock on to the streets, taking the aromatic air, heading across the river to Sachsenhausen ...

Where the bars and eating houses are packed and strident, tables clustered with bodies, drinkers straggling out into court-yards and on to footpaths, lifting glasses to each other under trees and awnings. On the roads and bridges the traffic is thick and slow – cars hooting, drivers draped out of windows to shout, greet, abuse. Every kind of vehicle nudging through the streets or abandoned at every conceivable angle and in spaces that only outlandish imagination and rampant optimism could transform into parking spots. From one of these niches a red Mercedes is being towed away supervised by two policemen and cheered on by an appreciative audience some of whom, having wandered across from nearby bars, are in a mood to toast the hapless (and, of course, absent) owner, the police – who remain stoutly oblivious – and anyone else taking their fancy and attention.

Our party of eleven, led by Rudolph, Wolfgang and Kristiana who know 'the ground', is pressure packed into two Volkswagens and eventually released into this throng after some characteristically inventive parking. With five days of conference sessions successfully behind us, we are ready to relax. And so, catching the mood, we wander from bar to bar, seeking one not so crowded, rejecting this one, sampling Sachsenhausen's traditional drink, *Apfelwein*, while summing up that one, returning at last to the first choice, 'The Painted House.'

Late as we are and genially doubtful though the waiter is about the chef's tolerance, we are eventually served an enormous, redolent pork dish. Ten of them in fact, and a small Wiener Schnitzel for Wolfgang who says that a heavy meal would interfere with the drinking of dark beer which apparently is a something that has to be undertaken later on. With the food comes a huge pitcher of the inevitable apple wine – it looks like an awful lot but slips down dangerously well. The pitcher is emptied and replenished almost immediately.

Around us, and for that matter among us, the atmosphere is riotous: songs and shouting and foot-tapping and table thumping resonate round the room sometimes dropping by sheer chance into booming concord, but mostly rising to the raftered roof in splendidly raucous dissonance. Through all this the waiters pilot the huge jugs of wine and sweep up the empties with a speed and panache that endangers nearby plates, heads and ever more expansively gesturing arms. Our waiter keeps us well supplied, tells us we'll be drunk for a week, accepts a quick glass now and then, and donates half a jug left over at another table.

We foreigners agree, as we raise yet another glass, that the apple wine is beautiful to the taste but has almost no affect at all. We concede, however, that none of us has as yet attempted to stand up, so when Paddy sets off bound for the toilet his progress – which involves a more or less forward movement complicated by the apparent necessity to rebound off nearby objects or bodies – is watched by all of us with great interest and a concern that is *almost* sobering. Though not finally sobering. Not remotely.

Thursday, 26 March: very early morning
Sometime between midnight and one, with our own table and one other still rollicking along, our waiter asks, 'Have you no beds to go to?' and a slow, reluctant, chaotic exit gets under way. Back out in the street the air is still balmy though a little chillier which helps the apple wine, that we had so confidently decided was domesticated to start getting its own back. The neon signs have become blurry and hard to read and the footpath seems uneven. Effects no doubt of fatigue and the lateness of the hour.

We mill around amicably in the roadway. Some jokes are told which are without doubt among the funniest I have ever heard and some songs are sung so harmoniously, with such accord and understanding between the tunefully interposing voices (some of which are contributed in brief snatches from passers by) that it is just simply a crying bloody shame that no one recorded them. Meanwhile, though we don't seem to have been actually *going* anywhere, we have arrived at another bar where, Wolfgang announces, we must now drink the dark beer. Somewhere, a long way back in my head, a voice murmurs that the dark beer will probably turn out to be a mistake. But even as I am puzzling over this introspection we are flocking through the strangely narrow doorway of the bar, claiming one of the long wooden tables and decisively ordering steins of the dark beer. Which turns out to be excellent, ridiculously light and unthreatening and having, as we all agree several times, very little effect at all.

The bar is dingy, cacophonous and full of smoke. From where we sit – at a table on a sort of raised platform at one end of the long room – we are able to survey the whole scene. Conversely, the whole scene can also survey us which it does for a minute or two with, in general, distaste and, in the case of one group, outright and vocal hostility. Rudolph says loudly that this behaviour is an insult to the Australian visitors and that he is left with no choice but to personally beat up all three men in question. Kristiana dissuades him and the idea seems to disappear as quickly as it emerged, to the visible disappointment of the three intended victims.

Gradually the sensation of our entrance dies down and everyone returns attention to the dark beer and various other interests – increasingly torrid homosexual embraces at one table, just as ardent heterosexual entwinings at another, a temporarily abandoned but now fully reactivated dispute at the bar ...

The staff look like they'd had enough hours ago and move about deftly but with a resigned sourness that is crazily at odds with the growing frenzy of the clientele. For my part, though I notice these dramas unfolding, I am more engrossed in a conversation of extreme seriousness that I am having with Volker, Bruce and Syd, a conversation in which we share personal and professional confidences of a kind rarely volunteered even among close friends: unquestionably, among the clouding smoke and the battering noise, one of *the* important conversations of my life. Though I can't actually recall what exactly it was about and what finally we decided.

It is perhaps half past two when the head barman – a squat grim bloke some several axe-handles across the forehead – invites us to leave. We do so with considerable dignity, thanking him for his hospitality, a courtesy which, inexplicably, seems to enrage him. Syd attempts to shake his hand but his conciliatory gesture is impatiently ignored.

Somewhere, whether in the bar we have just left or at The Painted House or on the crowded footpaths, we find we have lost three of our number. The remaining eight of us – Wolfgang, Syd, Paddy, Volker, Kristiana, Rudolph, Bruce and me – stand in the middle of the street, most of the traffic (though to make it exciting not quite all of it) having dwindled away. Several of us laugh and joke brilliantly and hug Kristiana whose slim silhouette and flowing flaxen hair would make the heart race if excesses of alcohol had not already induced such palpitations while simultaneously rendering quite academic any other ideas one might vaguely have entertained about Kristiana. But Wolfgang stands to one side trying to remember the whereabouts of a bar he knows that stays open till four in the morning. There we can drink the light ale, though, he warns, it is a particularly rough and unsavoury place and 'we will almost certainly have a fight.'

We straggle down this street and that, only Wolfgang paying attention to directions – which turn out so consistently to be wrong that he finally asks help of a man and his girlfriend, two of the very few people we now encounter in the Sachsenhausen byways. The man knows where the bar is. He refers to it as 'the bonecrusher', is incredulous that we intend going there and says we will undoubtedly have a fight. Nevertheless, he tells us the way and somewhere about three o'clock we make another grand entrance into what Wolfgang has described to us as a haunt of criminals, prostitutes, pimps, theatricals, academics and other unsavoury denizens of the night. At this stage though, it would have to be assertively loathsome for us to see it as anything other than great fun.

The walls are festooned with hay rakes, horse collars, old fashioned hoes and other antique rural instruments as well as artistically braided ropes and wheatsheafs. Black-coated, bow-tied waiters of vast muscular development patrol the packed tables and the stand-up bar, shuttling endless glasses of light-amber, very frothy beer to a clientele that seems to range from thoroughly bourgeois to definitely seedy. There are more of the latter than the former.

But while we vaguely take all this in, laughing randomly and competing well with the noise level which is stupendous, our central mission is the light ale to which, at Wolfgang's particular insistence, we now address ourselves. Fortunately, though it has been a long night, we are in fair condition to appreciate it. Certainly there is *some* falling about. True, Rudolph tips slowly backwards out of his chair, giggling casually. True also that one of my emphatic gestures to illustrate an anecdote sweeps a full glass off the table and under an adjoining bench. But these are aberrations: in a *general* way, we are ready for the challenge of the light ale.

In the dense, smoky atmosphere nobody takes much notice of what is happening around them (one man even subsides quietly and with no fuss to the floor without rousing the interest of anyone outside his immediate party and even their concern is brief). We have, however, attracted the attention of a black-haired evil looking bloke and his slit-eyed, unsmiling mate who are looming over our table from the crush of people at the bar. Black hair borrows a cigarette lighter from our table and tosses it back without thanks. His girl arrives and they kiss long and hard while his mate buys her a drink. She is blonde, striking like her boyfriend, but a bit too ravaged. When *she* borrows the lighter she returns it with an elegant, 'Thank you so much'.

Somehow her presence, alternating between her two toughs at the bar and us at the table, all the time creating and delighting in tensions and uneasiness, seems to speed everything up. Events seem bent on amounting to something, coming to a point. It's as if we've become part of a fiction.

Blondie is smiling brilliantly, waving her cigarette, 'just loves Australians', is very attracted to Paddy and proves it by sitting on his knee (in the background Black-hair's amused indulgence changes to bleak restiveness and his offsider looks absolutely murderous). *Blondie drinks from each of our glasses, orders more beer ('the Australians will pay'), shouts, 'Give me some fire' waving a fresh unlit cigarette at the lighter. Volker is singing a folk song, I am telling jokes in an Indian accent, Syd is discussing a test match from the past with Bruce. Paddy's arm goes round Blondie and Black-hair, who seemed not to be looking, knocks it away and his charming mate leans in closer. Things hotting up everywhere. Three men stand up and square off nearby. A chair goes over. Blondie downs two full glasses of our beer and the mate takes a third. Bells are ringing four o'clock and waiters are rushing last orders through the mobile crowd. Volker is arguing furiously with our waiter who says we have paid too little, Blondie asks Kristiana for twenty marks and smiles disdainfully when politely refused. 'More light ale,' shouts Wolfgang being shunted backwards out the door. 'Watch your pockets', warns Syd gnomically.*

And then we're back on the streets yet again, effortlessly swept clean from the bar by the muscular waiters: up above, no stars now, and a cold breeze blowing fine rain as we start the long walk home. The cars are out of the question and will be abandoned where they are until tomorrow when Wolfgang and Kristiana will be fit to drive.

And so we walk, becoming quieter and quieter, saying our goodbyes and going our various ways at the bridge over the Main. Through gleaming, commercial Frankfurt, footfalls ringing absurdly in shopping malls and squares: Syd, Wolfgang and me. At five we are near 'home'. Blackbirds are waking all over the city, limpidly tossing questions and answers from post to post, tree to tree, housetop to housetop.

The rain settles in, cold and insistent.

Thursday 26 March, just about dawn, and spring, for the moment, has been and gone in Frankfurt and Sachsenhausen.

[When the dynamic Anna Rutherford revived the European Association for Commonwealth Language and Literature Studies (EACLALS) she invited, among others, Syd Harrex and me. We gave papers, did readings and generally contributed as substantially as we could over a period of about eight years to EACLALS conferences in Spain (Sitges), Malta (Valetta) and Germany (Frankfurt). All of these conferences were outstanding and, for Syd and me, thoroughly memorable for all kinds of good reasons. In saluting Syd with this recollection of one of our many adventures together, I must also record with sadness the passing of two of our great friends and colleagues who shared that conference and many others with us: Anna Rutherford and Bruce Bennett.]

The Trespasser

ADRIAN CAESAR

'All poetry is trespass', you said,
so I leapt over your fence with words
into the fields of youth again
where I heard tweed-suited parody,
a gamekeeper, gun crooked over arm,
with the inevitable Labrador,
'Hey you, stop do you know
whose land you're walking on?'
Cocky, I said, 'Lord Pilkington's
and this is right-of-way not crops.'
'No, this 'ere's Lord Derby land
and you're a trespasser,' he said,
'Don't let me see you 'ere again
or the police'll have you next time.'
My mouth zipped anger in forever –
fields and trees were not for me
but the sherry set with landrovers,
and I thought of Nan at twelve leaving school
for the Mill and Will her husband
volunteering for trenches.
Lord Derby's scheme approved of that
and other kinds of sacrifice;
no wonder as a man I left to seek
this 'paradise' for the working class,
where now I find I'm on another's land again
but ask no leave from the dispossessed
to enjoy my suburban ownership,
this quarter acre block,
and do not see slaughter in deserts,
the hanging prisoners in their cells,

or hear the last croaks of a dying tongue,
saying take me back to my own land,
but instead inscribe in black
this frail apology of verse –
a hope that some day we might agree
to allow all people trespass.

Notes on Contributors

Ron Blaber is the head of Department of Communication and Cultural Studies in the School of Media Culture and the Creative Arts at Curtin University. He has a teaching and research background in Postcolonial and Australian Literary Studies. His recent work examines the relationship between Popular Narrative and the Social across several media.

Murray Bramwell taught English and Drama at Flinders from 1972 until his retirement in 2010. He is currently the Adelaide theatre reviewer for the *Australian*.

Anne Brewster is Associate Professor at the University of New South Wales. Her books include *Literary Formations: Postcoloniality, Nationalism, Globalism* (1996) and *Aboriginal Women's Autobiography* (1995). She co-edited with Fiona Probyn-Rapsey a special issue of *Australian Humanities Review* on whiteness (2007). She has published articles on whiteness and Aboriginal literature in *Journal of Postcolonial Writing*, *Australian Literary Studies*, *Feminist Theory* and *Journal of the Association for the Study of Australian Literature*. She has book chapters which use experimental approaches to writing about whiteness in *The Racial Politics of Bodies, Nations and Knowledges* (2009) eds Barbara Baird and Damien Riggs and *Practice-led Research, Research-led Practice in the Creative Arts* (2009), eds Roger Dean and Hazel Smith. She has also published the innovative writing using the methodology known as fictocriticism.

Adrian Caesar was formerly Associate Professor of English at UNSW@ADFA. More recently, he has split his time between teaching creative writing part-time at ANU and writing full-time. He is the author of several books of literary criticism and his non-fiction novel, *The White* (Picador, 1999) won the Victorian Premier's Award for non-fiction and the ACT Book of the Year in 2000. His poetry has been widely published and includes four books, including his latest publication *High Wire* (Pandanus Press, 2006).

Julian Croft was born in Newcastle in 1941 and educated there. His initial training was in documentary film in the Commonwealth Government's Department of Interior Film Division. Following that he has taught in universities in Australia, West Africa, and Austria. He retired from the University of New England in 2001 and is currently Professor Emeritus of English at that University. His first poems were published by Max Harris in 1962 and he has been publishing since then. He has produced four books of poems, one novel, and a co-authored music drama, as well as books of literary criticism and biography, and editorial and bibliographic works. He lives in Armidale NSW, and his latest novel will appear in 2013.

Trevor Fennell is Emeritus Professor in the Department of Language Studies at Flinders University. He is a noted scholar of Latvian language and literature.

Md Rezaul Haque is a PhD candidate in the Department of English, Creative Writing and Australian Studies at Flinders University. He teaches English linguistics and English-language literatures in the Department of English, Islamic University, Kustia, Bangladesh. He is co-editor of *The Shadow of the Precursor* (Newcastle-upon-Tyne: Cambridge Scholars Publishing, 2012), a *Transnational Literature* sub-editor and a poet.

Rick Hosking recently retired from the Department of English, Creative Writing and Australian Studies in the School of Humanities at Flinders University, where he worked in all three areas. He is managing to maintain his research interests in historical fiction and in writing an historical novel.

Susan Hosking is a Senior Lecturer and Postgraduate Co-ordinator in English and Creative Writing at the University of Adelaide. Her particular interests are contemporary post-colonial fiction, film and cultural studies. She has published extensively on Australian literature, Indigenous life narratives and literary and cultural representations of life in Australia, increasingly in a global context.

Brian Matthews is honorary Professor of English at Flinders University South Australia, where he taught from 1969 to 1992. He is the award winning author of *Louisa* (Penguin 1987; UQP 2001), and *A Fine and Private Place* (Picador 2000). His biography of historian Manning Clark – *Manning Clark A Life* (Allen and Unwin 2009) – won the National Prize for Biography in 2010.

Sudesh Mishra was born in Suva and educated in Fiji and Australia. He is the author of four books of poems, including *Tandava* (Meanjin Press) and *Diaspora and the Difficult Art of Dying* (Otago UP), two critical monographs, *Preparing Faces: Modernism and Indian Poetry in English* (Flinders University and USP) and *Diaspora Criticism* (Edinburgh UP), two plays *Ferringhi* and *The International Dateline* (Institute of Pacific Studies, Suva), and several short stories. Sudesh has also co-edited *Trapped*, an anthology of writing from Fiji. Sudesh is working on a fifth collection of poems, a collaborative project on popular Hindi cinema (with Vijay Mishra) and a series of papers on minor history. He is currently Professor in Literature, Language and Linguistics at the University of the South Pacific.

Satendra Nandan is an award-winning writer and has authored and edited more than a dozen books and numerous articles and papers on a variety of subjects including Literature and Politics. He has been an Adjunct Professor at the Humanities Research Centre, ANU, and the Centre for Applied Philosophy and Professional Ethics at the CSU, ANU, and Melbourne. Satendra was made a Professor Emeritus of the University of

Canberra in 2005, for his scholarship, writing and service to the University. He joined the University of the South Pacific in 1969 and resigned in May 1987 to join the Bavadra cabinet in the Labour-NFP coalition Government of Fiji. He was elected to Fiji Parliament in 1982 and 1987. Professor Nandan left Fiji in December 1987 to take up a fellowship at the Humanities Research Centre, ANU. Subsequently he joined the University of Canberra, ACT, and resigned in December 2005 to return to Fiji with his wife Dr Jyoti Nandan to help establish the University of Fiji in Lautoka and became the Foundation Dean and Professor in the School of Humanities and Arts. He was the elected international chair of The Association of Commonwealth Literature and Language Studies (ACLALS) and the Foundation President of PEN International, ACT. He is also the foundation Chair of the Fijian Writers Association.

Vincent O'Sullivan is an esteemed New Zealand poet, fiction writer, and editor. He is also noted for his critical work and scholarship. He has received numerous distinguished awards, residencies and fellowships, and his writing has been widely published nationally and internationally. Collections of his short fiction followed a number of collections of verse, and O'Sullivan has written for radio, television, and the stage. In 2006, he was awarded $60,000 for poetry at the Prime Ministers Awards for Literary Achievement. From its inception, Vincent O'Sullivan was a staunch supporter of CRNLE.

Kirpal Singh is an internationally acclaimed poet, scholar, critic and writer and recipient of numerous awards and grants. Singh is a presence in the global world of letters and is also known for his passion for Creativity & Innovation. In Singapore Singh is regarded as a cultural and literary icon. Currently Singh is with the Singapore Management University where he is Director of the Wee Kim Wee Centre and where he also teaches Creative Writing and helms the newly introduced Arts and Culture Management Program.

Paul Sharrad teaches postcolonial writing at the University of Wollongong. He completed all his degrees at Flinders University, his doctorate coming to fruition under the care of Syd Harrex. Paul worked for some time in the Centre for Research in the New Literatures in English (CRNLE) and was the founding editor of the *CRNLE Reviews Journal.* Since then he has published books on Raja Rao, Albert Wendt, and Indian English fiction, edited work on Kate Llewellyn, Pacific literature and textiles and texts, edited *New Literatures Review* and currently is the New Literatures editor for *The Years Work in English Studies.* His very occasional poetry has been published in Australia, Hawaii, New Zealand and India.

Ron Shapiro (Shepherd) taught in the English Department at the University of Western Australia. His research interests include New Literatures in English and Australian Literature, especially Jewish-Australian writing. He was a key figure in the early foundation of CRNLE notably in his editorship with Kirpal Singh of *Patrick White: A Critical Symposium* (1978)

Helen M. Tiffin, until her recent retirement, was Professor of English at the University of Tasmania. She is regarded as a significant and an influential writer in post-colonial theory and literary studies. She was formerly Professor of English and Post-Colonial Studies at Queen's University in Canada. Prior to her move to Canada, Professor Tiffin held the post of Professor in the School of English, Media Studies, and Art History (EMSAH) at the University of Queensland where she was a founder member of the Postcolonial Research Group. Apart from her interests in colonial and postcolonial settler cultures, Helen Tiffin is a keen artist.

Graham Tulloch is Matthew Flinders Distinguished Professor in English at Flinders University. He has written extensively on Scottish literature and is the editor, or co-editor with Judy King, of a number of scholarly texts, including Walter Scott's

Ivanhoe and *shorter fiction*, James Hogg's *The Three Perils of Man*, published by Edinburgh University Press, and Marcus Clarke's *His Natural Life* published in Oxford World's Classics. In more recent years he has also undertaken research on the reception in Australia of Scottish literature, particularly the work of Burns, Hogg, Scott, and Stevenson, and on the connections of Scottish writers with Australia.

Wakefield Press is an independent publishing and distribution company based in Adelaide, South Australia.
We love good stories and publish beautiful books.
To see our full range of books, please visit our website at
www.wakefieldpress.com.au
where all titles are available for purchase.

Find us!

Twitter: www.twitter.com/wakefieldpress
Facebook: www.facebook.com/wakefield.press
Instagram: instagram.com/wakefieldpress